IN CELEBRATION OF ELASTIC WAISTBANDS

Episodes of Imperfection, Insanity, and Occasional Enlightenment

CHRISTEE GABOUR ATWOOD

Christee Gabour Atwood

IN CELEBRATION OF ELASTIC WAISTBANDS

By Christee Gabour Atwood

IN CELEBRATION OF ELASTIC WAISTBANDS

Copyright ©2010
By Christee Gabour Atwood

All rights reserved. No part of this book may be reproduced in any form or by any means without prior written consent of the author, except for the inclusion of brief quotations used in reviews or by leprechauns, sasquatches, or wayward dust bunnies.

ISBN 978-0-9713420-1-9

Library of Congress Control Number: 2010914024

Printed in the U.S.A.
Rubber Chicken Press
P.O. Box 82423
Baton Rouge, LA 70884

DEDICATION

To the incredible groups of friends I have shared elastic moments with throughout my life – including:

- the Four Musketeers
- the Three Laser Beams
- The Friday Whine & Cheese Club
- the Girls Night Out Gang
- the Baton Rouge Algonquin Table (BRATs)
- the Thirsty Thursday Drinking & Writing Club
- my Writing Muses
- the Gabour and Atwood Krewes
- as well as other, more socially acceptable organizations that allowed me to be one of their members…

It took half a century for me
to truly appreciate what friendship means
in making the good times last
and helping the bad times pass.

And they've helped me realize that
there are only two kinds of people in the world –
Friends I have …
and friends I have yet to make…

✷★✶✵✴⬥✵✷
If God had intended for me to stay one size,
he wouldn't have invented elastic waistbands....

CONTENTS

The Elastic Waistband Society 1
1. Guidelines for Elastic Living 4

Accidentally Running Over my Bathroom Scale ... 22 times 7
2. The Dessert Cart on the Titanic 8
3. A Stick by Any Other Name 11
4. Flu-Like Symptoms and Epiphany 13
5. The Battle of My Bulge 16
6. Life, Liberty, and the Pursuit of Chocolate 18

We're All Turtles on Fenceposts 21
7. Friends Before Breasts 22
8. The World's Oldest Profession - No, Not That One! 25
9. Secrets of a Happy Marriage 28
10. Thank You, Mr. Blue Car 31
11. Perfect is in the Eye of the Beerholder 33

Work and Other Four-Letter Words 37
12. Fun at Work ... How To Change Jobs Without Really Trying 38
13. Workplace Slanguage 41
14. Everything I Know About Work, I Learned From Television .. 44
15. Dopey, Grumpy, Sleepy, and Me… 47
16. The Office WorkForest 50

My Inner & Outer Kids Are Having a Slapfight 53
17. My Inner Child is a Dishonored Student 54
18. Living on Borrowed Time 57
19. The Power of Pink 60
20. Updating My Cootie Shots 63
21. Memories of PCU* (*Pants that Covered Underwear) 66

People I've Met & Missed... and Associated Restraining Orders.. 69

22. I Wish I Had Known Eleanor 71
23. Benny "Da Bomb" Franklin and Me...................................... 74
24. My Close Personal Acquaintance, Dave Barry....................... 77
25. But UnSeriously Folks 80
26. A "Finer Than Frog Hair" Gentleman.................................... 83

A-Parent Insanity 87

27. The Sunday Afternoon"Will Cheat for Chips" Poker Club...... 88
28. Elderly Woman Thwarts Would-Be Purse Snatcher 91
29. Throw Mama From The Bridge.. 94
30. Starting the Next Ninety-Seven Years 97
31. My Mother's In My Mirror… 100

Hit and Miscommunication 103

32. And, On The Eighth Day, A Committee Created The Camel..104
33. Don't Try This at Home 107
34. Working With Customers …
    Or Holding A Cardboard Sign By I-10 110
35. The Five Questions You Should Never Answer 113
36. I Got the Most Points … in Golf... 116

Domestic Violets.. 119

37. Mr. Clean Goes on Vacation 121
38. Losing Found Time... 124
39. Cat Toys, Hairballs, and Other Pursuits
    of the Superior Species 127
40. Television, Internet … and Cold Turkey............................... 130
41. My Cat Is More Popular Than I.. 133

Families, Clubs, Cults … The Leery of Relativity.................... 137

42. The Atwoods and 2.5 Cats.. 138
43. All Grown Up But Not Dead Yet 141
44. A Club Is Born, Dies, and is Reincarnated........................... 144
45. The "Doctor, It Hurts When I Do This" Association 147
46. The Ack!-ARP Card 150

In Celebration of Elastic Waistbands

Attitude Altercations 153

47. Zen and the Art of Nothing 154
48. Happily Ever After ... After What? 157
49. Being Happy Ruined My Life 160
50. Taking a Humor Inventory 163
51. What Else? 166

**A Writer's Life: A Dog's Life Without
That Interesting Ability to Lick Oneself 169**

52. Overnight Success ... The Fifty-Year Method 171
53. Writing a Book in One Month and a Few Fifths 174
54. How to Write a Column 177
55. National Novel Writing Month, a Chicken Suit,
    and Myron 180
56. Virtually on Tour 183

Couching the Idea of Therapy 185

57. Pressure ... It's Not Just For Cookers Anymore 186
58. Being Assertive – If That's Okay With You 189
59. An Impostor With Restless Leg Syndrome 192
60. This Tape ... and My Reputation ... Will Self-Destruct 195
61. The Expense of Being Brilliant 198
62. Side Effects of Christee 201

Failure ... Makes Great Stories for Late-Night TV 205

63. Failing Your Way To Success 207
64. Lessons From a Chagrined Capuchin 210
65. Principles and Vices of Principles 213
66. Journaling, ADHD, and Shiny Objects 216
67. I Prefer to Give My Age in Dog Years 219

Balanced & Unbalanced Lessons 223

68. Thinking, Rethinking, and Drinking 224
69. The Balancing Act 227
70. We Are Not Alone 230
71. Refrigerator Box Redecorating 233
72. The Cynic's Quiz 235
73. Never Watch a Saints Game with a Priest 238
74. Lessons I Still Haven't Learned 241
75. The Moral of these Stories 244

✺★✴✷✵⬟✹✺
If I laugh at myself first,
then the rest of the world
is laughing with me, not at me.

Introduction

THE ELASTIC WAISTBAND SOCIETY

I am the proud founding member of the *Elastic Waistband Society*.

I am starting this society because I've realized that, while it is important to stay healthy, it's also important to give ourselves a little leeway for the occasional times when other things take priority.

So while I'm residing in the "elastic end" of the closet right now, I know that it's only a visit, not a permanent address.

This period in my life has helped me recognize that there are times when we need to give ourselves permission not to be perfect ... and nothing does that more than the perfection of elastic waistbands.

These are the magic tools that allow us to be size 12 when, in all honesty, a size 14 would be more appropriate. These are the tools that show us how items can be stretched as needed and then, when the time is right, happily returned to their original size. And elastic also allows us to make full use of our investments at all-you-can-eat buffets.

This book celebrates those elastic times. It laughs at my misadventures in the hope that it will make you feel better about yours. It ensures that you know you're not alone in the dark end of your closet, whether dealing with inches or issues. Your elastic friends are right here with you. And we've probably brought brownies.

What else do I, as the founding member of the *Elastic Waistband Society,* believe?

I believe that...

- A single waist size is the sign of a stagnant mind.
- Laughing at myself is an effective exercise.
- Seeing my feet can be done with a mirror.
- Exercise has caused more injuries than couches.
- Airbrushed model's figures are not good goals unless we also have airbrushed lenses on our glasses.
- Thomas Hancock, the inventor of elastic is the most brilliant person since Mr. Einstein, and that Hancock's birthday should be made a national holiday. (A side note here: He originally named the machine that created elastic the "pickle" so no one would know what it was and steal his invention... Brilliant, I tell you, brilliant...)

- ✭ Being comfortable in a size 14 is more important than being miserable in a size 10.
- ✭ Supersizing can be just as much fun for me as it is for my drive-thru order.
- ✭ A big number on the bathroom scale is a temporary condition, but a big heart is forever.
- ✭ And finally, I believe that elastic is the perfect invention. It shows flexibility, a willingness to grow or tighten up as needed, and that giving myself a little breathing space is not necessarily a bad thing.

So there you have it. The tenets of the Elastic Waistband Society.

We're proud. We're strong. And we're elasticized. Bring on the "all you can eat"…

This year I will stop considering Oreos as one of the major food groups.

Chapter 1

GUIDELINES FOR ELASTIC LIVING

I've created my own list of guidelines to help me stay focused in my elastic lifestyle.

These are things that I can use to measure my activities to see whether I should have taken a left turn at Albuquerque.

I'm listing them here in case you'd like to use some of these to create your own list of guidelines. That's because the first guideline is to avoid reinventing the wheel. But it's not on the list because I already told you...

So, before I add any more guidelines, here we go...

1. I will put on my oxygen mask first.
2. I will accept that sometimes life feels like I'm on the Titanic armed only with a tablespoon.

In Celebration of Elastic Waistbands

3. I will take expert advice with a grain of salt. After all Mr. Frankenstein was a doctor.
4. I will realize that work is a four-letter word without the same satisfaction.
5. I acknowledge that I'm only as old as I feel in my mind and there are no wrinkles in there.
6. I will enjoy the fact that romance is not one-size-fits-all.
7. I will not use an eraser. I will learn from – and revel in – my mistakes.
8. I believe that if God had meant for us to stay one size, he wouldn't have invented elastic.
9. I say, "Let the one among us who has never merged poorly, honk the first horn."
10. I realize that trying to manage time is like trying to put a tutu on a pig.
11. I will appreciate conflict. Without it, we'd be writing our emails on stone tablets.
12. I will never use the phrase, "Stop acting like a child."
13. I will stop spending time at "whine and cheese" parties.
14. I will try something new each day unless that *something* includes a bungee cord and a bridge.
15. I will look for heroes who don't wear capes.
16. I will accept that other people can make me angry once, but only one person makes me stay that way.
17. I shall celebrate the fact that there is really no such thing as "normal."
18. I will show off my warts so that they can't embarrass me.
19. I will always expect to fall upward.

20. I will stop to smell budding roses, newly cut grass, and old books.
21. I know that whatever doesn't kill me will make a great story. (And the thing that does kill me will probably make one too – just not one that I'll write.)
22. I realize that life is not spent on the balance beam, but rather the seesaw.
23. I accept the fact that pets, not CEOs, are the superior species.
24. I will be myself. If I don't, there's a leftover name badge in the world.
25. I know that one person's failure is another person's sticky note.
26. I will learn that "No" doesn't require an explanation.
27. I will seek a lesson and a laugh in every story.
28. I will speak positively and carry a rubber chicken.
29. I will celebrate my successes, my failures, and my wrinkles.
30. I will not be embarrassed to be a fan.
31. I will enjoy being well-insulated.
32. I will stop looking for shortcuts and revel in the journey.
33. I will never regret a laugh line, cheering for a losing team, or a bite of chocolate.
34. I will never stop learning ... and unlearning.
35. To be continued...

Some weasel took the cork out of my lunch.
-W.C. Fields

ACCIDENTALLY RUNNING OVER MY BATHROOM SCALE... 22 TIMES

This section addresses our constant preoccupation with the bathroom scale.

This preoccupation causes us to try the scale in several locations, different rooms, and at various angles before getting the lowest possible weight.

We go through eras where our weight on that scale is the most important thing to us.

Then we go through times when the weight in our heart is what matters. And both times are equally vital to our survival ... no matter what the designers say as they continue to make clothes that look good only on birch trees.

Does this section apply to you? Answer the following questions:

- Have you ever tried a diet with the word *cabbage* in the title?
- Do you find yourself continually buying new bathroom scales because "this just can't be right"?
- Do you think exercise is not as much fun as a barrel of monkeys?

If you have ever described yourself as "big-boned," this section is for you...

Chapter 2

THE DESSERT CART ON THE TITANIC

One of my favorite quotes of all times is from my hero, Erma Bombeck.

She said, "Seize the day. Remember those women on the Titanic who waved off the dessert cart."

This sums it up. I need to enjoy every moment. I need to savor every breath ... and every bite...

I can see myself at the pearly gates saying, "Hey Peter, you could have given me a little warning on this. Do you realize I passed up a perfectly good fudge brownie delight today? Do you think I would have done that if I had known those pounds wouldn't count?"

Do you know whom I envy the most? Not skinny, healthy, athletic women. No, I admire 'big-boned' women who wear bikinis. Yes. There's healthy self-esteem for you. No apologies. No excuses. They are my new role models, not those waif-like blondes sporting their new Nikes on my exercise videos.

Me? No such esteem. Every pound creates a new exercise in futility. I share these frustrations with my husband.

"David, the bathroom scale is messed up again."

"We could get a new one. That one hasn't been the same since you dragged it behind the Toyota."

"Maybe. I mean, that number can't be right. You don't think I could be that huge, do you?"

"Define huge."

Wrong answer.

So, while David enjoys his time outside of the house, I try to remember my confident moments. Those moments when I was not obsessing about my weight. But the last one was in 1983 and its memory is fading quickly.

Then I do what I always do when I am running out of room at the elastic end of the closet. Yup, it's back to SugarBusters.

First, I throw away the sugar in the house. Then, I get rid of the potatoes. I check to be sure all our bread is whole wheat. And finally, I stare in the freezer at the Triple Chocolate Chunk ice cream. And then my real battle begins.

"David, we're not supposed to waste food. Throwing this away would be wasting. There are people starving in ... in ... well, where is there a deprived spot in civilization?"

"Your parents' house?"

He's really hitting a lot of wrong answers today.

When he gets back into the house this time, I am still staring at the ice cream. "I just don't know what to do. I can't afford the temptation, but it only has a few scoops missing."

"And think of all the baby chocolate chunks that had to die to give us that ice cream." He has his baseball cap over his heart.

I sigh sadly. "And a cow had to give up the milk."

"A tree gave its life for the packaging."

"An advertising person sweated to come up with the slogan *It's good*."

We looked at each other, with tears misting our eyes. It was the poor advertising person that got to us.

"How wrong it would be for us to slight all those who gave of themselves so that we could experience this triple chocolate chunk ice cream," I whispered reverently.

We got rid of the ice cream. Unfortunately, we did so by eating it. But the knowledge that we had honored all those who had suffered for us made me feel much better as I threw away the defective bathroom scale.

I believe that cheesecake and Prozac
share many of the same healing qualities.

Chapter 3

A STICK BY ANY OTHER NAME

I was in the store the other day looking at exercise equipment. Don't laugh. I buy it. I just don't use it.

As I was browsing through these instruments of torture, I made an amazing discovery. I could buy a stick.

Yes, it was labeled as an "exercise bar." But it was a stick. A stick with which to exercise. A stick that came in many different weights. But it was a stick nonetheless. And instantly I knew there must be other similar discoveries to be made, so I went in search of them.

I felt the thrill that I'm sure Lewis and Clark experienced as I came upon my next item. A block. It was a plastic block, sturdy enough to stand on. It was called an aerobics step system. But it was definitely a plastic block. I realized that I have one of these amazing "steps" on my front porch, made of the more durable concrete material.

This was getting really exciting.

I found a book on walking. All this time I thought I had mastered this walking thing by the age of two. But a quick glance through this book made me realize that I've been doing it all wrong. Apparently I'm supposed to burn extra calories while walking by flinging my arms as if I'm being attacked by hordes of Girl Scouts trying to sell me Thin Mints.

Next I saw ankle weights. Apparently you strap these around your ankles when you work out. Quite honestly, the reason I need to work out is the fact that I have added weight around my ankles... along with many other places. Why do I need to buy these when I have my own weights already built in?

I also found a huge ball that you roll around on. Wow, this certainly seemed like a good idea. I know that there weren't nearly enough opportunities to hurt myself while just rolling around on the floor. Thank goodness someone found a way to make floor exercise just as dangerous as bungee jumps.

I even discovered these new fancy "gliding discs." Basically it looked like you were supposed to stand on these frisbees to exercise. Yeah, this is a good idea. Just about as good an idea as that time I tried changing a light bulb while standing on my rolling desk chair.

But, do you want to know some good news? The exercise section of the store led right into the lawn and garden area. And there it was. The answer to all my exercise woes.

I didn't buy anything. Instead I went straight home and pulled out this great exercise machine that let me work out and get my yard cut all at the same time. What will they think of next?

※★※★※●※※

I'm a well-insulated girl.

Chapter 4

FLU-LIKE SYMPTOMS AND EPIPHANY

Last week I had some of those mysterious flu-like symptoms that the athletes always have when they don't want to go to work.

And they changed me into a new person.

For nearly a week, I wasn't able to hold onto food, liquids, or coherent thoughts. It was a nice vacation. And all I could think at the end of that exhausting week was, "Hey, I lost five pounds! If I could just stay sick one more week I could wear a size smaller!"

And when I realized I was well and would have to eat solid food again, I got depressed. Believe me, with me, sick is better than depressed. Depressed means I sit on the couch, shout Latin epithets at my cats, and lament over the fact that it's too far down to the ground to retie my shoelaces.

I also took the time to listen to my inner voice again. Not good. That girl is crazy.

"I can't believe you think you need to eat again. You ate this morning."

"Well, it's okay to eat more than once a day. The surgeon general said so."

(By the way, it doesn't matter who says which one of these statements. In case you hadn't figured it out, they're both me.)

"So, you're well enough to get to the couch. Why don't you exercise?"

"I had a high fever just yesterday."

"You always have a flimsy excuse like that. Just like the time you held up traffic just because there was a really, really sad baby spotted owl that had wandered away from his mommy on Christmas Day. Or the time you said you couldn't do your air shift at the radio station just because you had lost your voice."

When she resorted to telling old radio stories, I finally couldn't argue with her anymore. I headed to the treadmill.

Fifteen minutes later I was talking to Grandma as I walked on the treadmill. No problem there. Well, okay, one problem. Grandma passed when I was in high school. But besides that little detail, the exercise session went pretty well.

A few minutes later, as I lie on the floor waiting for a stewardess to appear from nowhere with an oxygen mask, I realized that I'm treating myself poorly again. I say wonderful things aloud, but inside there are all sorts of strange conversations going on.

I say, "I'm happy with myself. I don't mind that I have to wear elastic waistbands all the time."

Inner Me says, "Yeah, I'm proud that with only seven pounds more, I'll have enough mass to create my own magnetic field and begin attracting small satellites into orbit around me."

I say, "I like me."

Inner Me laughs, "Hey, I also like Beverly Hillbilly reruns. So, why should 'liking me' surprise anybody?"

I say, "I'm going to treat myself as well as I treat other people."

Inner Me says, "Or at least as well as I would treat a terrorist, Dick Cheney, or somebody carrying an Amway case."

So, my latest goal is to be nice to me.

"You hear that, self? I'm going to say something nice to me every single day."

"I'm waiting."

Here I go… "I may not be smart, but I hide it well by smiling a lot."

Yup. This is going to be harder than I thought.

I use my exercise bike ... as a coat rack.

Chapter 5

THE BATTLE OF MY BULGE

It's happened again.

I have expanded my horizons in ways that I'd prefer not to expand. And I have realized that they're right when they say, "De Nile is not just a river in Egypt anymore."

A few years back I went on a streak of exercise and dieting and got down to a weight that I wasn't embarrassed to admit on my driver's license. However, this last time when I renewed my license I said, "Leave that weight on there." I could swear I heard hysterical laughter behind my back as I left the DMV.

When I had lost my excess weight I got rid of the fattest end of my closet and only kept one size of clothing bigger than my standard size. Now, refusing to buy a size larger again, I have moved into the "indeterminate size zone."

This special size classification includes buying clothes one to two sizes too small ... with lots of elastic. And buying one-size-fits-all clothes. And trying to create "expanders" for waistbands that no longer work correctly. (Expanders are often called safety pins. They are used when the button and the buttonhole of a waistband refuse to see eye to eye.)

There are many other consequences to this stage of my weight gain. I refuse to look at my full-length mirror because it looks like I'm in one of those carnival mirrors. I avoid photos because they make my cheeks look like a chipmunk. And I make excuses for visiting the dessert bar by saying things like, "I'll make up for it by just eating salad tonight."

Yeah. Right. Salad.

I decided I'd like to avoid those gentle reminders people in my family are bound to start giving again. "My, aren't you looking well-fed." Or "When are you due?" Or "What's that noise?" when we both know it's the sound of thighs in corduroy meeting more insistently than they should.

And so, I am doing it again. I am headed back to the gym. I am dusting off my collection of diet cookbooks. And just in case that doesn't work, I'm going shopping for a new pup tent to add to my wardrobe.

※★✳✷✳●✳※

Yes, I've heard that the definition of 'delusion' is "sucking in your stomach when you go to stand on the scale". In my defense, that's pretty much the only way I'm going to be able to read the thing.

Chapter 6

Life, Liberty, and the Pursuit of Chocolate

As I stand, looking from one side of my closet to the other, I realize that my clothes tell a story.

My clothes range in size from 8 (as long as I don't want to use those pesky buttons) to 14 with elastic (okay, okay – 16). And, while I am not thrilled with the upper extreme, I also realize that I don't want to hang around that lower number either.

Size 8 was never any fun for me. It was a world that was lacking many important things, such as:

- Life ... because breathing is not possible for me in size 8;

- ✤ Liberty ... because movement is hampered so that items above shoulder height are as unattainable to me as a good hair day; and the
- ✤ Pursuit of happiness ... which can mean only one thing – chocolate.

Yes, chocolate has played a major role in my life. When removed, I have become more irritable, moody, and subject to "fits of expression." When properly applied, I'm a more kind, more gentle, and more ... well, more me. For those who know me as normally irritable and moody, the idea of a gentler me is quite appealing. So, for holidays, friends, family, and psychiatric professionals ply me with chocolate. Wise, wise people.

I remember as a child, I created my own incentive system. I would reward myself with one square of a Hershey Bar every time I finished a section of my reading. Amazing concept, wasn't that? It started out with one little square for every chapter. But that wasn't quite enough. So, then it was a square for each section of the chapter. Then it moved to a page, a paragraph, and finally, I started giving myself an entire Hershey Bar for just opening the book. I grew in size, not in knowledge, with this system.

I remember visiting Baskin Robbins for the first time and honestly asking the man, "Why do you waste time with the other 30?"

I remember a world where there were two flavors: chocolate and chocolate with something else in it. I thought a vanilla shake was simply a shake where someone had forgotten to put in the syrup.

So can you imagine my thrill when I realized that there was a month with a holiday that seemed expressly designed so that people could give each other boxes of chocolate? I worked hard to have boyfriends in February so I could cash in on this tradition. That didn't work, so I compensated by creating my very own holiday. I celebrate February 15th, the holiday where those reduced-price heart-shaped boxes of chocolate are always plentiful.

And so, next time Valentine's Day rolls around, I hope you get lots of dark chocolate. And if you don't, I'll see you in the stores as we search for good bargains and good moods, compliments of February 15th – Cheap Chocolate Day.

Yes, laughter is the best medicine.
Boxed wine is running a really close second.

WE'RE ALL TURTLES ON FENCEPOSTS. WE DIDN'T GET HERE BY OURSELVES.

I love this saying. I feel like this is the updated version of "No man is an island."

This section is populated with stories that remind us that, no matter how amazing we are, we weren't born that way.

We are a gumbo made up of the people we've learned from, the examples we've followed, and the mistakes we've made, combined with the latest fashions from the sales rack.

And you know what? All those mistakes and wrong turns have made us the people we are today. And those people are pretty amazing.

Does this section apply to you? Answer the following questions:

- Have you ever wondered how "self-made" men were born?
- Do you know there's no "I" in team, but there is a "me"?
- Is your idea of a really good day any day that you don't end up in the police blotter?

If you're still holding this book, this section is for you.

Chapter 7

FRIENDS BEFORE BREASTS

After thirty-something years I finally reconnected with friends from my elementary school days.

And I made some realizations.

There are some words that can only be shared with those you knew before you had breasts. (Gentlemen, add your own comparable experiences. I won't even try…) Yes, there are things that can be said only to friends from the time before you knew how to hide your warts. To people you could ask what "that word" meant. To people you envied and loved at the same time.

The funny thing is to talk to these friends decades later and realize that they thought you were okay. This seems strange since all you remember is being embarrassed because everybody else seemed normal and you felt so abnormal. It's even more amazing when you realize that they felt the same way.

What a joy. What a release. What a wonderful discovery. And now I realize – what perfect timing.

Our group of four musketeers got together for the first time in over thirty years last summer. We rediscovered each other in person, by email, and by phone, and realized that the very things that drew us together as young compatriots were still there. That we actually liked each other as adults. And that we had someone to talk to when tragedy fell. And it did.

Our artistic musketeer's tragedy fell when she discovered that her marriage was over. And she picked right up and amazed us with her strength. She cursed a little, dusted off her feelings, and began to build a new life. The girl is beautiful inside and out, and has reminded us that being part of a pair is nice, but being a whole person is essential.

And then, the unthinkable. The musketeer with the biggest heart got the call that no one is ever prepared for. Her soulmate – and a gentler, kinder, more supportive soul I've never met – had left his heaven on earth with her and was moving on to his next adventure. This reminded the musketeers what it meant to be there for each other. And just as we would have guessed, she put herself into taking care of others at the local food pantry instead of insisting that she needed to be taken care of. The phrase 'steel magnolia' comes to mind...

Thank goodness our lifeline musketeer has been on duty through all of this. She's the evergreen vine that keeps the musketeers connected. So, while the rest of us get lost from time to time, we know this musketeer will always be ready when we find ourselves again. She remembers to be there for us even when there's not a tragedy to remind her. What an incredible gift...

Then there's the last musketeer. She gets lost a lot. She's busy chasing rainbows that aren't as pretty when she catches them. And she forgets what's important, but she's relearning. She is remembering why these musketeers make life worth living even when the tragedies fall. And she realizes that the other musketeers might even need her a little. She knows she needs them and she won't lose them again.

One for all and all for one, my friends.

✯★✴✳✶✦✷✯

Winning the biggest and most expensive toys is not the most important thing. After all, how much fun is a seesaw without a friend on the other side?

Chapter 8

The World's Oldest Profession...
No, Not That One!

I was invited to speak at a teachers' conference. It made me stop and think about the world's "oldest profession".

I know the other profession you're thinking about. But no, teaching is older. Because nothing in this world happens without first learning how to make it happen.

The invitation brought to mind some of the poor souls who had the job of trying to teach me.

There was the teacher who had to explain to me that making one finger stick up was a not a socially acceptable gesture. She also explained that I should never use that signal again unless, later in life, somebody cut me off in traffic.

Then there was my sixth grade teacher. Believe it or not, in those days, I was timid and shy about speaking. It was he who discovered my passion for cats and got me talking about that in class before I realized what I was doing. I had never really spoken out in class. But I was suddenly arguing about why cats were superior to dogs. I had spoken my opinion aloud! And nobody died! And then I did it again. And again. And now look. No one can shut me up. Yes, you have this man to give the credit ... or blame.

There was also my tiny, elderly, genteel English teacher, the first teacher I allowed to read one of my teen angst poems of how I was the only person in the world with my particular problems. And she encouraged me. She taught me that you could say something in a very few words and still have a giant impact.

Then along came my Latin teacher, who taught what everybody called a "dead language." She taught it with pride. Unfortunately the only Latin I seem to remember now is the phrase for, "Don't let the little 'varmints' get you down." (You can replace the word 'varmints' with whatever term you prefer.) She developed my sense of pride. From my one Latin phrase I learned that what other people think doesn't matter. I am the one who decides what's important in my life.

And there was my college history teacher. He acted out scenes from history in class. We snickered. We thought it was silly. But we listened because he usually carried a big stick when he performed those acting jobs. More importantly, we remembered. From him I learned that, if you're willing to ignore your ego and concentrate on getting the message across in any way you need to, you are a true communicator.

Those are a sprinkling of the lessons that I learned through years of association with outstanding teachers. And today there are dedicated teachers out there teaching more and more lessons to more and more kids. And for that, we, your lifetime students, can never thank you enough...

✦✦✦✦✦✦✦✦

We should not permit prayer to be taken out of the schools; that's the only way most of us got through.

-Sam Levenson

Chapter 9

SECRETS OF A HAPPY MARRIAGE

You would think, with a title like that, that I actually know the secrets of a happy marriage.

But no. I don't think there are real secrets. I think we just have to figure out what works for us ... and realize that those aren't the same things that sound great on a greeting card.

For me, it helps to recognize the stages of a marriage. Discovering those patterns can be quite useful as you laugh hysterically over the concept that the two sexes could hope to live together in harmony.

Let's take a look.

The first week of a marriage is wonderful. You have all that money people have given you. You have all those toys that came as gifts. It's Christmas and you know how nothing else matters on Christmas morning? That's where you are.

Alas, Christmas passes and the bills arrive. The stages are a little different after that.

The first seven years are spent trying to make your mate more like you. Why? Because we spent all that time dating pointing out the ways we're alike. "Oh, you like sushi too? We are so much alike!" So, we want to extend that feeling. Of course, that becomes difficult since we exaggerated things during dating. "I love ESPN too" should have been translated, "I'll watch ESPN if I have a good book to read while it's on." So, we're trying to reinvent our spouse in the image we created in dating days. Now there's a great recipe for disaster.

The next seven years start with the realization that we don't really want someone who is just like us. So, instead we start trying to change our spouse into our ideal person.

This is the time when that trait we loved them for in the beginning becomes the enemy. That easy-going, laid back personality becomes a "lack of ambition." That "energetic, focused person" becomes "obsessive." We spend seven years before we discover that we really did like those traits that attracted us in the first place. If we make it through this stage, we're either doing great or we've been in a seven-year coma.

Then comes the fifteenth year. I think this one is the cardboard anniversary, isn't it? (Yes, mine is a discount marriage.) Some marital concepts start to suffer. A good sex life becomes accidentally bumping into each other in the hall. A conversation usually has no pronouns.

"Ready?"

"Yeah."

"Want to do Chinese?"

"Fine."

This stage may be misinterpreted as the "I'm married to my sibling" stage, which is a totally different thing in the hill country. But if we look more deeply, we realize that our focus has shifted off the other person and onto ourselves. That's when we start seeing that the changes we want in other people are actually reflections of what we want to change in ourselves. And we have to realize that our spouse is going through the same process.

This is the time when we discover that we're married to a person who has different interests. We have to date them again and figure out how those interests mesh with ours. In other words, we have to start the whole doggone process over again.

And I wouldn't have it any other way.

Hey David, I love ESPN ... with a book.

Things happen.
Words are said.
And before you know it, somebody's throwing a mime off a bridge ...
                                    -David Atwood

Chapter 10

Thank You, Mr. Blue Car

You turned around my entire day today and you don't even know it.

You waved me into traffic and smiled. And suddenly I felt human again.

Let me explain why this was such a big event.

The day started as usual. I struck the alarm clock with the side of my hand. I forgot that I had put a spoon from my cough syrup on top of there last night when I awoke at 2 a.m. with a coughing fit.

So, it is 6:00 a.m. and a spoon is doing a gentle arc across my bedroom. Thank goodness it didn't hit anything important. The swelling on my husband's nose is expected to go down in two to three days.

I make my way to the coffee. Unfortunately, somehow I have set it for 6:00 p.m. instead of a.m. and I have to wait for it to brew. By standing in the kitchen for this period of time, the cats and dog have now all decided it is time for them to be fed. Then there is the obligatory 15 minute period standing in the doorway to the back yard trying to decide if they want to go out or not. A gentle boot in the rear decides that they all opt for the fresh air of the outdoors.

I get into the shower and realize that I have forgotten to get shampoo so I am squeezing what is left out of three different hotel shampoo bottles. I go to choose my outfit and discover that the extra pounds I have put on limit me to either wearing a mumu my sister brought back from Hawaii, a maternity dress that I got at a garage sale as a joke, or a small army surplus pup tent.

As I try to choose the right shoes to go with camouflage, I realize that I have six pairs of hose with at least one run in every one. Why I have kept these, I do not know, but I quickly realize that I will have to twist the run to the inside and walk like I have a pulled leg muscle all day to keep the torn spot from showing.

Because the idea that things couldn't get any worse is always foreign to me, I find that someone has run over my mailbox during the night and I have to prop the mailbox up on a step stool so that the postman won't refuse to deliver my mail addressed to Occupant.

My car was running on fumes and I had to stop, even though I was already late. So now I smell like premium unleaded instead of Tea Rose Parfum.

And then, there you were. It was a simple wave and a smile that you gave to tell me you'd let me into your lane. And suddenly, a middle-aged woman with twisted hose, a camouflaged outfit, and a confused mailman had a good moment. I smiled the rest of the way to work.

You have no idea what you did…

✯★✷✹✷♦✹✯

The true measure of a man is how he treats someone who can do him absolutely no good.
-Samuel Johnson

Chapter 11

PERFECT IS IN THE EYE OF THE BEERHOLDER

The thing I get asked most often by people who read my magazine columns is, "Is your husband really that perfect?"

And I have to answer, "No. But he's perfect for me."

Because what makes one person happy is what drives another one crazy. Otherwise, all women my age would be married to the same man. And I don't think that's legal, except in Utah.

But my poor man understands me. Let me illustrate.

I remember the day I had been writing for hours and forgotten the most important word in the computer world – "Save". The computer froze and I was using every curse word in the English language, as well as a few from my Arabic forefathers, when I looked up and saw a piece of duct tape hanging from the center of the doorframe. At the end of the duct tape dangled a king-sized Hershey Bar. Need I say more?

Then there was the time when I was completely depressed (we writers have to have our angst, you know) and I plopped down on the couch to growl at the television. He came to sit next to me. And suddenly, seated between us, there was a new addition to our family. A sock puppet named Guapo appeared, introduced himself in some unidentifiable accent, and immediately began to make rude remarks about every person on television. When he got to the point of describing a rear end as "two boars fighting in a grass sack", I couldn't stay depressed any longer. Guapo has been living with us for about a decade. He often accompanies us to sporting events and dinner with my brother's family. Strange that no one else invites us to dinner.

Then there was that period when I was infatuated with kicker Morten Andersen, during his days with the Saints. Did my husband get upset? Did he laugh at me? Well, yes, he did laugh, but no he wasn't upset. Instead, for one of my birthday presents, I found that the man had gotten Morten to sign a picture and had it framed for me.

When my best friend, a 17 year-old cat with a missing tooth and a torn ear, passed away, did he treat it lightly? No. He cried with me and then we drove two and a half hours with a frozen cat in the back seat so I could bury her next to my 13 year old cat from childhood – my earlier best friend.

When I was president of a humane society and we had a house filled with thirteen cats, two dogs and a parrot with an attitude, did he ignore the fact that we saw an injured owl in the middle of the road? No. He took one look at my

In Celebration of Elastic Waistbands

distressed face, pulled the car over, and started directing traffic until I talked the bird into getting in the car with us.

When we went to an LSU basketball game that didn't have many people in attendance, was he embarrassed because I stood through most of the game and cheered at the top of my lungs? No. Later that night when we watched the news and they commented on the "small, but lively crowd," he just smiled and said, "That's my girl. A small, but lively crowd." And I think he was proud.

Twenty-something years ago on May 28, a skinny girl in a hoop skirt and a long-haired boy who played drums in a rock 'n' roll band walked down the aisle. They were surrounded by a small, but lively crowd of dear friends. Three months later they moved to Los Angeles with nothing but second-hand wicker furniture and a handful of dreams. Over the years they've sadly lost some of those dear friends and thankfully most of the wicker. They've been broke and felt rich, they've learned hard lessons and great jokes, they've gained pounds and lost hairs. And they did it all together. To me, that is perfect.

Happy Anniversary, David.

My idea of a good day is any day where I don't glue the back of my hand to my forehead.
                                                                -David Atwood

✯★✶✹✵⬢✵✯

I want my children to have all the things I couldn't afford. Then I want to move in with them.

-Phyllis Diller

WORK
AND OTHER FOUR-LETTER WORDS

This section addresses the major portion of our lives that we spend in a workplace saying "TGIF."

We realize that we only have jobs so we have something to complain about when our personal relationships are going well.

Sometimes we think that some of our jobs are more important than other people's jobs, but then there's a garbage strike and we realize how important every job really is.

This section muses on how great it would be if each of us recognized the importance that every job has to our lives and remembered to play nicely with others in the workplace.

Does this section apply to you? Answer the following questions:

- Do you go to work to get a nap?
- Do you list your former employers as "Jerk #1, Jerk #2?"
- Do you have a resume that looks like *War and Peace* ... without the peace?

If you have ever asked, "Is it 5:00 yet?" this section is for you...

Chapter 12

Fun at Work ... or "How To Change Jobs Without Really Trying"

It happens to me pretty regularly.

I look in the mirror and I'm wearing the basset hound expression. I sigh deeply with each breath. And every time the phone rings, I find myself quoting Dorothy Parker with "What fresh hell is this?"

It's the blues, depression, mood swings – whatever you want to call it. And I, like many basically normal people, find myself sinking with changes in the weather, the stages of the moon, allergy season, my unbalanced chemistry, or any other excuse my mind can come up with. And my husband, being the astute observer of human nature that he is, can tell at first glance when I am in one of those moods.

He looks over as I am doodling pictures of tombstones and quietly asks, "Is something on your mind?"

I look at him. Now, I love this man. But at a time like this, there is nothing good that can come out of my mouth. So I answer, "The futility of life. The uncertainty of the future. The fact that the only things in the closet that I can wear are your clothes."

He knows that there is only one thing he can do for me. He backs away, scrambles onto his Harley, and gets away as fast as he can.

When I'm in a mood like this, there's nothing that someone on the outside can do for my insides. And that's why I started looking for the things that make me smile, that bring me back from that dark place, and that make me less likely to force unwitting telemarketers to listen to my latest problems with allergies.

I find that I'm not alone. Many others share these dark moments. That's why today I offer my favorite Fun At Work Ideas. These are ways to recover your sense of humor, your sense of lightness, and yes, even your ability to laugh at political commercials.

- Have a sock puppet give your presentation at a staff meeting. (Be sure she's wearing earrings. Trust me, sock puppets just look better with earrings.)
- Add the following disclaimer to all your memos and emails: Offer void in Canada and Dayton. Licensed drivers only.
- Wear a rubber chicken around your neck and when people ask why, just say, "What rubber chicken?"
- On your Microsoft Word documents, go to the File menu. Click on Properties. Go to the Summary tab. In the Title line, type, "If you are reading this, you have too much time on your hands."

- ✯ Put your wastebasket on your desk and label it "In Basket".

- ✯ Put up a sign on your cubicle that says, "Midlife Crisis in Progress. Enter at your own risk." Watch how quiet your day becomes.

- ✯ Answer your phone like an answering machine. Tell them to leave a message, make the beeping sound, and then hang up before they have a chance to speak.

Disclaimers for this chapter:

- ✯ Use at your own discretion.
- ✯ Void where inhibited.
- ✯ Should not be used at jobs to which you are particularly attached.

✯★✶✳✶●✶✯

When asked how many people worked in the Vatican, Pope John XXIII (1958-63) is said to have replied: "About half, I think."

Chapter 13

WORKPLACE SLANGUAGE

Communication in the workplace.

It's very much like a game of grapevine when we were kids ... and a little less effective.

The boss comes in and says, "Everyone needs to straighten their work areas. The CEO is coming by."

This news is taken in by the department heads and disseminated to the managers. "The CEO is coming over to inspect the office."

The managers tell the supervisors, "The Board of Directors is considering huge cuts and layoffs. They're sending the CEO to every department to assess the situation and see who's dispensable around here."

The supervisors leave that meeting and give the information to their employees, "Everyone needs to straighten their work areas. The CEO is coming by."

Okay, sometimes it all works out. But more often, it seems like we are all speaking different languages in our offices. And I believe that's where the biggest problems in the workplace arise. Well, that and the fact that those of us who don't have "indoor voices" operate poorly in cubicles.

Here are some examples of that special "slanguage" of the workplace.

- "The meeting is scheduled to begin at 8:00." That seems like a simple enough statement. However, in some companies that "scheduled to begin" is just a suggestion. I realize this as I sit there at 9:15 with the guy from IT who just came for the doughnuts.

- "We're like a family around here." The actual translation is "We're just as dysfunctional as your family, including your Uncle Pete who insists on wearing that silver lamé dress to Thanksgiving dinner each year."

- "We've always done it that way." This is not an explanation. This is a threat. Lions roar. Bears growl. Long-time employees just say, "We've always done it that way." You have been warned.

- "Your report was great, but…" Actually nothing after the "but" matters. "But" is the word that means you are about to be slammed. "But" means, "I was just softening you up for the kill."

- "What an interesting idea." This means your idea was so ridiculous that they can't even think of a good enough way to make fun of it. In this case, consider yourself the winner and enact a hasty retreat.

Then, if you move from the cubicle to the boardroom, there are conversations that don't make sense no matter how you translate them.

"You have to sit to the right of the head of the table to be in the 'power' seat."

I watched the guy on the left squirm, "I thought it was the left."

"No, I'm pretty sure it's the right."

Another guy joined in, "What's this year's power color?"

"Red again."

The teal ties fidgeted uncomfortably.

"What if a person in a teal tie sits to the right of the head of the table?"

They all just stared. I knew it was just a matter of time before they started debating who would win if a person in a teal tie had a slapfight with a red tie person at midnight on New Year's.

Pig Latin has nothing on Workplace Slanguage. And it makes more sense…

✯★✳✵✸✹✺✫

An expert is a man who tells you a simple thing in a confused way in such a fashion as to make you think the confusion is your own fault.
-William Castle

Chapter 14

Everything I Know About Work, I Learned From Television

On my brother Bob's birthday, we found ourselves discussing the television we watched in our formative years.

Three channels, rabbit ears antenna, shades of gray, and no remote control. Nobody wanted to sit close to the television in those days.

It wasn't because of all the warnings about radiation. It was because you then became the "human remote control." The words, "Christee's closest to the TV," brought fear to my heart.

But that little box was powerful. We learned so many things about life from it. Let's think back to some of the television lessons we learned about the workplace.

We watched *Gilligan's Island*. Skipper's method of disciplining his employee was to hit him over the head with his cap. And we won't even talk about the issues that come into play with the fact that he was always calling Gilligan, "my little buddy."

We had *Bewitched*. Larry Tate's way of impressing clients was to fire Darren in front of them. He'd yell, "Darren, you're fired." And then he'd sneak around and rehire him when he needed the work done.

What about *Star Trek*? Every time there was hazardous duty it was the new member of the staff who was thrown to the wolves. Captain Kirk would say, "We're going to the planet's surface. It will be me, Spock, and the new guy, Rubinowitz." And when they got to the planet, he'd say, "I'll check out that rock. Spock, you check out the plant life, and Rubinowitz, you check out that big snarling monster with the twelve sets of teeth." Rubinowitz never got to say a word. Guess they didn't want to pay the actor scale.

Mr. Ed. When an architect has his office in a barn with a horse that is smarter than he is, do you really want him to design your home?

There was the *Dean Martin Show*. Dean Martin was never seen without a glass in his hand. Substance abuse right there in front of us. And we don't even need to discuss the existence of his group of dancers called the Golddiggers.

Remember *Hee Haw*? It was one of those shows that made us see two types of women. Those girls in the tight outfits who stood in the cornfield and acted dumb ... and Minnie Pearl. Those were our two choices for role models? Needless to say, I went with Minnie.

Remember when we were shocked by the things Archie Bunker said on *All In The Family*? Kind of pales when you think of *South Park*.

Thank goodness today's generation is growing up with ideals based on quality television and high standards like the sophistication of Jerry Springer, the camaraderie of *Survivor*, and the morality of the Hilton sisters.

Uh oh, I just scared myself...

✯★✶✹✷●✷✩

I really hate my boss. She gripes at me constantly. She pushes me too hard. And she never believes my excuses when I call in sick. Self-employment is tough.

Chapter 15

DOPEY, GRUMPY, SLEEPY, AND ME...

Human Resource departments never get a break anymore.

They have harassment cases, violence issues, and discrimination cases to deal with everyday.

It made me start thinking that, if things had been like this in the days of our youth, our childhood tales would have been totally different.

The Seven Dwarfs alone would have been an HR nightmare. First of all, they, of course, would have been the Seven Little People.

Dopey would have been immediately singled out for drug testing. Doc would have been in court for practicing without a license. Sleepy would have been sent in for sleep testing. Grumpy would have been enrolled in anger management classes. Sneezy would have been on workman's comp for his condition. Bashful would have been moved to the IT Department. And Happy would probably have been the victim of workplace violence on a particularly bad Monday morning. Yes, it would have made for quite a different story.

And Prince Charming would have been an entirely different set of issues. This guy would have had so many sexual harassment suits against him that he would have had to travel with a full-time lawyer. After all, going around and kissing sleeping women, stealing women's shoes, slaying endangered species, and other such escapades would not have won him a princess. That would have gotten him ten to fifteen at Leavenworth.

And wasn't that Goldilocks kid just breaking and entering? The nerve of the girl. She goes in and steals people's food and complains about it? And then she tries to take over part of the house. I just feel like there's an in-law joke somewhere in there...

The three little pigs would have had so many code violations for the shoddy construction of their houses, that no one would have blamed the wolf for blowing the dumps down. In fact, he probably would have been awarded the contract for demolition for the rest of those fairytale places that didn't meet code – especially that tower where Rapunzel hung out. It didn't even have a fire escape. And that old woman in the shoe would not only have those code violations; I'm pretty sure social services would have been called in too.

Don't even get me started on cartoons. Did anybody else notice that Bugs Bunny was a cross-dresser? That Elmer Fudd was constantly picked on because of his speech impediment? And that those chipmunks were just darn obnoxious?

Today, it wouldn't matter if poor Casper was friendly. He'd be exorcised or chased by the *GhostHunters*. I'm sure George Jetson would sue the maker of that treadmill. Fred

Flintstone? He'd be in trouble with PETA for trying to put the cat out.

We won't even mention the fact that Jonny Quest looked like Race Bannon, the sidekick, instead of like his dad, Dr. Benton Quest. That's a column subject for another day.

Yes, it was much simpler then. I think all our problems started when Snidely Whiplash passed the bar...

✯★✳✴✳✦✴✯

Give a man a fish and he'll eat for a day. Teach a man to fish and he'll call in sick every time it's good weather.

Chapter 16

THE OFFICE WORKFOREST

Upon venturing in and out of the world of cubicles and boardrooms, I have discovered that the world of work is much like a forest.

And I've begun to do a study of the fascinating group of creatures that exist in that "Office WorkForest."

See if you recognize a few of these critters:

The Energy Vampire Bat
This is the person who can find the sow's ear in a silk purse. Yes, she can find something bad no matter how good the situation sounds.

"We're getting bonuses!"

Energy vampire bat response: "We won't get them next year."

If you tell an energy vampire bat you have a great new computer program that will save 50% of their data input time, that bat will instantly respond, "Great, now I'm going to get laid off."

The Martyr Mongoose

No matter how many hours there are in a day, you'll find the martyr mongoose working twice that number. And like the sacrificial character in the old movies who had to be left behind, the mongoose will always remind you that "It's fine, you can go on to lunch without me. I'll be ... cough, cough ... okay."

The Expert Elephant

At the beginning of a meeting, Elvin the Expert Elephant jumps in, "You know, we would do better at these meetings if you had fruit instead of doughnuts. We wouldn't suffer the sugar crash later on in the meeting."

Shirley notes, "Every time we buy fruit, we throw fruit away. No one will eat it."

"Did you know it takes 21 days to create a habit?" Elvin notes.

"So, do you mean we should have fruit for the next 21 meetings? We won't even have this group together for that long."

Elvin is already bored by this topic and has moved on. "Is this meeting going to take long? I have an important appointment in two hours."

At this point the chairman has had time to look over the membership roster. "Elvin, you're not even on this committee."

"Right. I'm just helping out."

After the chairman finishes pounding the shape of his forehead into the wood grain of the table, Elvin decides he's helped enough and moves on to assist other departments.

The Analytical Armadillo

This hunchbacked creature wanders the earth in search of data. It feeds on numbers, statistics, and reports from last year's failed projects. By spending all of its time gathering such information, it's able to avoid doing any sort of meaningful work. This creature can be recognized by its protective armor, also known as a clipboard.

The Beleaguered Basset

No matter how little work this animal actually has to do, it will always leave a pile of "stuff" on its desk in order to make it appear that it's overloaded with work. The problem with the basset is that since it's constantly talking about how overburdened it is, it never actually gets around to doing any of the things on its imaginary task list.

I'll continue my research and report back to you as I spot new species in the workforest. After all, this research is how I keep from doing any real work...

✯ ★ ✱ ✻ ✱ ✦ ✱ ✯

For entertainment, I like to turn around in the elevator and say, "I suppose you're wondering why I called this meeting."
The result is that either everyone laughs ... or I get the elevator to myself.

MY INNER & OUTER KIDS ARE HAVING A SLAPFIGHT

This section addresses the fact that many of us feel like cast members from the movie *Alien*.

We look normal on the outside, but there's something inside us fighting to get out. But it's not a little green creature from another planet.

It's a tiny version of us wearing a comedy arrow through its head.

And, while society and the dress code at work restrict us from wearing that arrow on our head and the accompanying superman cape, we feel a constant pull to ignore convention and sniff a new box of crayons in the store.

Does this section apply to you? Answer the following questions:

- Have you ever wanted to run away to summer camp and leave the kids at home?
- Do you ever look through books and put them aside, saying "not enough pictures?"
- Do you have a really, really good answer for the question, "Why don't you grow up?"

If you took the time to look at these questions, this section is for you...

Chapter 17

My Inner Child Is a Dishonored Student

Yes, my inner child is a dishonored student at the school of hard knocks.

Once upon a time I thought I would be an adult by this point in my life.

Over time, I realized that growing up wasn't working for me. Growing up involves those things a real "grownup" does. You know, the kind of person who discusses his 401K, party politics, and impressionistic art. As it is, I still use a piggy bank for my retirement fund, wear my old "Pat Paulsen for President" button, and prefer crayons in primary colors.

How do I know that I can't grow up? Well, you decide…

- ✯ I read the funny papers first. Then I forget to read the rest of the newspaper.
- ✯ I'd like to build a tent out of sheets and hide in it.
- ✯ Bodily functions still make me giggle.
- ✯ I long to go to summer camp and create some more of those potholders out of stretchy bands of material.
- ✯ I'm writing this column with a cat on my keyboard.
- ✯ My idea of fine literature includes the word "muggles."

But I think there are many of us who would like to return to the ways of childhood. We want to laugh until milk comes out of our noses and squish a buttercup into somebody's face. We want to tell that person at work that he's being a big bully and if he doesn't quit we're going to have our big brother beat him up.

I'd like to reinstate some of the rules of childhood as rules of adulthood. Here are my proposed guidelines:

- ✯ Every afternoon, each of us should have a cookie and take a nap.
- ✯ If someone is rude to others, he or she should be forced to take a time-out in the corner wearing a silly hat.
- ✯ We should get a gold star stuck on our collar when we do something outstanding.
- ✯ After tough meetings, we should stand and shake hands with everyone in the room and say, "Good game."
- ✯ We should go to recess outside instead of sitting at our desks.

- We should change staff meetings into "storytime" and tell stories of difficult clients as big bad monsters.
- Instead of fancy performance appraisals at work, we should get report cards with extra points for good conduct.
- We should draw pictures of our achievements and post them on our refrigerator doors.
- And finally, every night, we should kneel by our beds and bless everyone in our lives who has made that day special.

This chapter is dedicated to the memory of someone who made lots of days special: My husband's brother Chuck (1956-2006). He followed the rules of a good childhood all his life. He beat up any bully who picked on members of his family, he loved recess outdoors, he told jokes to lighten up our darkest moods, and he even slipped us piggy bank money so we could have the Bridal Suite on our wedding night all those years ago. He will always be our honor student.

Laughter and tears are both responses to frustration and exhaustion. I prefer to laugh, since there is less cleaning up to do afterwards.
-Kurt Vonnegut

Chapter 18

LIVING ON BORROWED TIME

I shouldn't be alive.

I realized this as I watched children riding their bicycles past my house. They wore helmets, knee pads, and I think one of them had curb feelers on his tires.

I remember the safety equipment on my bike.

It was called the self-ejector seat. If something went wrong, and it usually did, you headed for grass and jumped. This was partly due to the fact that the bike was a hand-me-down from my older brother and much too tall for me. It was also because I knew that if I put on the brakes the chain would come off again. It is hard to look cool sitting at the end of your street, replacing the chain as traffic passes by.

I recall that, back in the '60s, we heard of a strange invention called a "seat belt," but they only had them in the front seats. They got in the way when I tried to sit on Daddy's lap to drive the car, so we sat on top of them.

I remember that we had a "crash test dummy" in our family. It was I. When my brothers and sisters needed to see whether their go-cart named "Old Junkie" would stay together in actual service, they would sit Christee on it and push it down the driveway into the street. Old Junkie never stayed together. I have the scars to prove it.

I remember being assigned as navigator by my sister who insisted that she could drive a bicycle with me on the handlebars. My entire navigation included 15 seconds of my screaming, "Mailbox at 12 o'clock!" before everything went dark.

I loved eating those suckers that had actual nickels in their centers and amazingly, I never once ate the nickel.

I knew that electricity and water do not mix even before huge labels were attached with the picture of the appliance and a giant red line through the bathtub. There was no need to tell me not to try to make toast while in a bubble bath.

I got burned by hot liquid without a single thought of suing.

I was attacked by a toy called a "clacker" when the huge acrylic orbs on cords wrapped around my wrist and bruised it to a lovely shade of purple. I even played "swing the statue" without a safety net.

We played stickball in the street and had a lookout who yelled "Car" so we could get out of the way in time. We ate Halloween candy straight out of our bags.

Of course, we weren't sophisticated back then. We were amazed by small things like watching the test pattern after the television signed off. We thought it was so great when we got our new weather channel, which was actually a camera that panned back and forth across an assortment of meters. And we never even noticed the string holding up the Starship Enterprise.

True, we weren't worldly-wise, but we were happy. We broke bones. We scraped knees. We burned off skin. We injured ourselves on practically every toy we owned, and we never blamed anyone but ourselves. We might not have been totally cured by it, but I'll put my mommy's kiss on my bobo up against any legal settlement any day.

Yup. I'm living on borrowed time. But I'm pretty happy about it...

✦ ★ ✳ ✱ ✱ ✦ ✱ ✦

We were smarter when we were children.
When we played, we played.
When we worked, like cleaning our rooms,
we worked.
And then we forgot about that work as soon as
we got back out into the yard to play again.
And we never once used the term "multi-tasking."

Chapter 19

The Power of Pink

The color pink has had an incredible impact on my life.

No, not because it is my favorite color. In fact, it is my least favorite color. My favorite is black, mainly because of the slimming effect.

It's not that I have anything against pink. It's just a case of "dislike by association." Pink is the color of Pepto Bismol, a necessary liquid at times of stress in my life.

But it was the color pink that made me realize I was different. It seemed that, in my younger days, every little girl loved pink. I remember when my Mom took me shopping at Sears & Roebuck and we looked at the cute little girls' nightgowns. Pink, pink, and more pink. I yawned until I looked across at the women's intimate apparel and saw a scarlet red shorty nightgown.

"Mommy, there it is!" I sounded much like a foghorn in those days – a tiny girl with the voice of Phyllis Diller.

"What's wrong, dear?" (Did I mention that my mother was much kinder to me in those days?)

"I see the nightie I want."

"Oh good." She turned toward the little Bambi outfit, smiling.

I ignored Bambi and ran across to grab the scarlet gown. Mom's teeth dropped. The attendant wisely disappeared.

"Christee, that's a grown-up gown."

"But I like it."

"Yes, but it's not appropriate for your age."

"But I REALLY like it."

She sat me down to explain that the gown wasn't quite right for a little girl. She stopped and waited for me to acknowledge that I understood.

"Mommy, I understand that it's a grown-up nightie. But by the time I'm grown up, it won't be here anymore."

You know, I think I stumped her. No, we didn't buy the nightgown that day. But on Christmas morning, it was under the tree.

I've had many other episodes with the color pink. My bridesmaids' dresses were pink. No, I still didn't like the color, but I worked right up to my wedding day, so my mother and sisters made those decisions for me. I think they chose that color just to pick on me, but that's only a suspicion.

I played the role of Shelby in a stage production of *Steel Magnolias*. I had to cut off most of my hair. No problem. I dyed my black hair blonde. No problem again. When did I have a problem? It was when I had to say the line, "Pink is my signature color." When I could deliver that line with conviction, I knew I was a good actress.

Recently I ran into a friend I haven't seen in years. She is a wonderful, caring woman whom I truly admire. And she was wearing a pink ribbon. She informed me that she is a survivor of breast cancer. She's trying to draw awareness to the disease with her pink ribbon so that others learn from her experience.

You know, maybe pink isn't so bad after all.

I am not young enough to know everything.
-Oscar Wilde

Chapter 20

Updating My Cootie Shots

"The man I marry will be special."

I smiled at the girl waiting in line to get a new set of piercings added to the two in her ears.

"Of course he will," I nodded politely.

"I'm looking for the perfect guy."

"What do you think would be perfect?" I was interested.

"Well, first, he has to be rich."

"Of course."

"I don't mean well off. I mean RICH. At least a couple of million."

"That sounds reasonable," I nodded, sliding my Gloria Blandertilt bag back onto my shoulder. "What else?"

"He has to have a good career, of course. I think he should be President."

"Wow. So you have political ambitions for him?" I was amazed she had planned this through so thoroughly.

"Oh yes. I think it would be nice to redecorate the White House."

"Good idea. I've heard the Lincoln Bedroom still has the same old bed Abe used."

"Well, we'll have to update that. I think pink and silver would be a nice change for that room."

"Sounds very different."

She held up a fuchsia painted fingernail and grimaced. "I broke this nail in computer class this week."

"That's too bad," I commiserated.

"That class is so hard. And my college testing has been a nightmare."

"Boy, you have a lot going on."

"Yes," she agreed. "Between school and dance class and yoga, I'm worn out. But I'm still out there husband-hunting."

"Good for you," I nodded as she moved up in line.

"And, of course, my relationship with my ideal man will not get in the way of my career."

"Well, good for you," I smiled. "And what is your chosen career?"

"I'm going to be a fairy princess."

Yeah, it sounded ridiculous. But I'm sure she'll outgrow it by her eighth birthday.

Kids are growing up so fast these days. They learn computers, talk about careers, and take tests to assure they're on track with their education. But when, during all of that, do they have a chance to splash around like fools in the rain, make necklaces out of clovers, build castles in the sand, and dislocate their shoulders while playing "Swing the Statue?"

Perhaps I'm sounding very naive here, but I'm asking the same question lots of people before me have asked: "When did we stop letting kids be kids?"

I guess that's the reason that I don't mind being a middle-aged kid. Could be that the younger generation could learn a thing or two from an older person who's not embarrassed to play. Sure, I embarrass other people around me, but I laugh a lot. And then other people start to laugh with me ... or at me ... but I prefer to think it's with me.

So, with my pet rubber chicken Elvis, I continue on in my midlife crisis, and I celebrate it by acting completely immature. But it's okay, we've had our cootie shots...

★ ★ ★ ✱ ★ ● ★ ★

That woman speaks 18 languages, and can't say no in any of them.
-Dorothy Parker

Chapter 21

MEMORIES OF PCU*
(*PANTS THAT COVERED UNDERWEAR)

I have hit the magic age of 50.

Yes, I know many of us insist on hiding our ages – but I am proud. I've earned every one of those gray hairs that disappear periodically with a little visit from Clairol Number 168. I've worked for those "laugh lines" and those pesky 35 pounds that come and go just often enough to keep me rotating between three sizes of clothes. And I've lived long enough to admit that there are times when the world baffles me, forcing me to retreat into my happy memories…

I remember:

- When the ultimate embarrassment was having your underwear show over the waistband of your pants.

- ✯ The day we discovered this new, fast-paced game called "Pong."
- ✯ Our family's black and white television with "rabbit ears" on top.
- ✯ The world's saddest funeral procession on television for a young president.
- ✯ Watching the death counts during the Vietnam War and each time trying to remember where my big brother was stationed.
- ✯ Working as a disc jockey and saying that FM stations would never replace popular AM stations. (I never claimed to be psychic.)
- ✯ Feeling perfectly safe trick or treating until the last house had turned out their lights.
- ✯ When neighborhood moms expected extra kids at the table for lunch. It was just accepted that you ate at whomever's house you ended up in at noon.
- ✯ The only times I couldn't control my voice while working in radio – when I was cursed at over the telephone for announcing that the king of rock 'n' roll had died; when I got a phone call that my old cat was going away; and when I heard the words "throttle up Challenger" on a small television we had at the radio station.
- ✯ When we took a nickel on our dates as "mad money," so that, if we got angry at our date, we could call our parents for a ride home.
- ✯ When a big night out for our family was driving through Dairy Queen for dipped cones, which became chocolate fashion statements as they dripped all over us.

- ✻ When people sent Christmas cards and actually meant the messages written in them.
- ✻ When the wording of the pledge of allegiance wasn't a problem. It was a promise.

I remember simpler times and sometimes I want to run back to them. But then I think of the incredible things that have happened since then, things I'd never want to give up. I've seen a nation grow closer in tragedy. I've watched the development of inventions that seemed like space age concepts become commonplace. I've watched once-feared diseases become footnotes in history. And I've grown to realize that the world is much larger if I open my mind to the possibilities.

I'm over 50. I love progress. I hate progress. And I still don't understand the definition of most of the words on the rest room wall. I guess I'm pretty normal.

I've reached that awkward age ... somewhere between "I've got it all together" and "It's all shifted one foot lower."

PEOPLE I'VE MET & MISSED... AND ASSOCIATED RESTRAINING ORDERS

This section considers the possibility that every life has one other soul that it would have benefitted from knowing.

Sounds pithy, and mind you this doesn't apply to those of us who want to meet some of the male models on the front of the steamy novels we hold a moment too long in the store before pronouncing, "Oh, I thought this was *War and Peace*. Silly me!"

No, we are talking about those people from other eras that we admire for their strength, their ability to communicate, or the fact that they could survive in a time before deodorant was readily available.

These are the people we hear about who did things we think are amazing and who make us feel just a little embarrassed about lying when filling out our profiles on alumni newsletters.

Does this section apply to you? Answer the following questions:

- Do you wish you had met Joan of Arc so you could have said, "Let's just keep that 'voices' thing between us?"

- ✱ Do you want to go back in time and hit Benjamin Franklin with an alarm clock for that Daylight Savings Time idea?
- ✱ Do you wish you could have beat up the writer who killed Bambi's mother?
- ✱ Do you wish you could have voted Eleanor Roosevelt into office?

If you are holding a book right now, this section is for you...

✱★✶✻✹●✹✱
It's such a thin line between
being a devoted fan and being a stalker.
I think the line is somewhere around the
point where you can identify the contents
of their trash can.

Chapter 22

I WISH I HAD KNOWN ELEANOR

My husband knows how to spot my "moods."

Normally, he wisely tries to escape quickly.

But today he pauses. It's that same pause of curiosity that makes our foot lighten up as we pass an accident scene. Or that amazement as our finger pauses on the remote before disgustedly hurrying past Jerry Springer. Whichever it is, today it is his undoing.

"David."

A combination of fear, adrenaline, and the "fight or flight" syndrome makes his voice go up an octave. "Yes?"

"What do you think of me?"

My hand is on his arm. I know that, for one brief moment, he thinks of chewing it off and running, but no, he is brave.

"I think you're a talented woman."

"Talented," I nod. "But not really smart?"

"Oversight on my part," he amends quickly. "Talented, intelligent woman."

"But no looks…"

"Talented, intelligent, beautiful woman."

"But my personality…"

"Talented, intelligent, beautiful, and friendly."

"But am I successful?"

"Talented, intelligent, beautiful, friendly, and successful."

He's having to count on his fingers to remember them all.

"But what is success?"

"And inquisitive too."

"You're just saying that."

"Well, I don't want anybody to get hurt." Yes, he's shielding our 17-year old dog.

"But what do you really think of me?"

"All of those things and more."

Gee, this guy is good.

He continues, "But what I think isn't important. It's what you think."

"I don't know what I think of me."

So, as he does when he wants to put me into a trance and escape, he poses a question. "Your assignment for today is to decide, 'What do you want to be remembered for?'"

I let him go. And I thought. Unfortunately I think best with Rocky Road. So I took a little side trip to the fridge. Then I thought.

I wanted to be remembered for helping, motivating, making people laugh. I wanted to be known for my compassion, and as a friend to animals. And on and on it went.

It was days later before it all came together for me.

In Celebration of Elastic Waistbands

I was watching a television special on Eleanor Roosevelt. Not a particularly attractive woman. The butt of many cruel jokes. And how dare a president's wife speak out on causes, no matter how worthy they were? She helped people even when others thought it was inappropriate.

I watched her bittersweet story and found myself whispering, "I wish I had known her."

And there it was. My goal. A mission statement for my life.

No matter what I make, where I go, what I look like. I just want people, years after I'm gone, to hear of the things I have done and whisper the words, "I wish I had known her."

✦★✶✳✵✹✷✦
Learn from the mistakes of others
because you can't live long enough
to make them all yourself.
-Eleanor Roosevelt

Chapter 23

BENNY "DA BOMB" FRANKLIN AND ME

I want to be like Benjamin Franklin.

He had such great quotes and in between being witty and insightful with his words, he was busy doing little things like discovering electricity, inventing bifocals, and creating the postal system so dogs would have someone to chase. He was a true renaissance man and he did it without being a particularly handsome guy.

I was discussing this with my husband the other morning as he tried to read the Sunday paper. He never gets to read a newspaper without me giving an ongoing commentary about the world.

"Another article about new inventions in here," I noted. "You'd think everything had been invented by now. I mean,

Benny Franklin probably invented more than the rest of the world put together."

"Benny?" He almost looked up from his paper. Or perhaps that motion was just his nervous tic. It's the tic that happens when I've talked over 65 minutes straight without taking a breath.

"Yes, I think we're enough alike that I have the right to call him by a nickname."

"Nice." He tried to hide his face behind the sports section. The poor man thinks if I can't see his eyes that I might forget he's there and stop talking for a nanosecond. He's wrong.

"I've decided that I want to be more like Benny. I'm going to focus on saying really witty quotes like he did all the time." I paused, but he didn't respond.

Like a lack of response would stop me from talking.

I thought for a moment and came up with my own quote. "Early to bed and early to rise. Damn that Daylight Savings Time." I giggled at my own joke.

No response. I was not thwarted. "Here's another one. If I were talking about someone really old, I could say, 'She's so old, that if she were a horse, she'd be holding painted macaroni rings to a paper plate by now.'"

I waited for a response. "Get it? Glue?"

I paused. No answer. "Are you listening?"

"Sure I'm listening. You're going to start saying witty quotes. When are you going to start?"

I was not amused. "I already said two of them."

"Oh, that's funny."

"No, it's not."

"You're right."

"Let me think." I concentrated so hard that my eyebrows met. Or perhaps that was the signal that a tweezing was in order. I finally came up with another one.

"How about this one? Always a bridesmaid, never a ... best man ... unless the surgery is successful."

He looked at me in shock. "When would you use that quote?"

"When I need to see if someone is listening to me. And it worked, didn't it?"

"Please tell me I'm not supposed to act impressed with these." He moaned to the classified ads.

"A picture is worth a thousand words," I said.

"Now that one's good. Not original, but good."

"I wasn't finished. A picture is worth a thousand words ... or a couple of thousand bucks if a motel, a call girl, and a politician are involved."

He didn't even make a noise. But what did I expect? Great genius is never appreciated in its own time.

Benny and I both know that.

Beer is living proof that God loves us
and wants us to be happy.
-Benjamin Franklin

Chapter 24

My Close Personal Acquaintance, Dave Barry

I went to New York City for BookExpo America, this incredible event where a bunch of authors, publishers, agents, and assorted insane people get together.

I needn't explain which group I fall in, right?

Even more special was spending time with my close personal friend and idol, Dave Barry. He was at the event signing copies of his new book and I was there begging people not to burn copies of mine.

We had a wonderful discussion, stopped to take a picture together with our buddy Ridley Pearson, and lamented the fact that people expect us to grow up when that's the last thing either one of us cares to do.

Yes, it was a very nice day.

Okay, in all honesty, I guess it wasn't exactly like that. Perhaps it went a little more like this.

"Next!" This was called by a young fellow who was given the job to protect Dave from strange people.

"The book is for your grandchild?" Dave jumped right into the conversation. He was going for the obvious, because his new book was a children's book.

"No sir."

"Child?" He looked doubtful as he stared at the gray hairs waving at him because my 'Clairol 168' had worn off.

Shaking of the head.

"Oh," he caught on. He smiled. "What's that name you want me to sign this one to?"

"Me."

"And who is me?"

I wordlessly pushed my nametag toward him. It was covered with the remains of a six dollar cola and a ten dollar bagel. Yeah. Convention center prices.

"That's K-r-i-s-t-y?" he asked kindly.

I nodded mutely. Now I know this is not the correct spelling of my name. They had mangled it atrociously on my name badge. But when Dave Barry says something, I am not going to disagree.

I choked and held up my camera, shaking it as I tried to speak.

"You'd like a picture?" Dave guessed.

Nod, nod, nod. I resembled an A-Rod bobble head in a low-riding Impala.

"Come on behind the table here and we'll get one taken for you."

I climbed over boxes, books, and stomped on Dave's lunch to get between him and Ridley and smiled as though I had just been poked with a cattle prod as the security fellow took our picture. Then I grabbed my book and hyperventilated the words, "Big fan."

"That's very nice. Thank you for coming by."

I tripped, took my book, and walked away with Dave's burger emerging from where it was now attached to my left tennis shoe. As I looked back I noticed that they had now doubled security at Dave's booksigning table.

Well, I guess he couldn't expect to get many more nice people like me so it was probably a good thing they were being careful to keep the crazies away.

On a non-related subject, just what is the definition of the term, "restraining order?"

✯★✶✹✦✹★✯
Scientists tell us that the fastest animal on earth, with a top speed of 120 feet per second, is a cow that has been dropped out of a helicopter.

-Dave Barry

Chapter 25

BUT UNSERIOUSLY FOLKS

I recently realized that I'm taking life much too seriously again.

This happens every so often when I start thinking that my resumé is nonfiction. That I might have useful information to impart. And that I understand the difference between "political correctness" and "beating around the bush."

In order to overcome this momentary delusion, I find myself quickly retreating into my past comfort zones.

I know that I subconsciously do this in order to ensure that I am not successful in any field that might be considered worthwhile. I know this because I passed a few of my college psychology classes. I've read mountains of self-help books. I've lain on a couch. (No psychiatrist there ... just a couch.) And I watched Jerry Springer once. (No, that last one has no bearing on the discussion. I just felt the need to confess it.)

And so, I'm thinking about running back to my sordid side. Yes, the world's second oldest profession. Comedy.

After all, no matter what has gone on in the world, there has always been a comic standing to one side, pointing out everything that the others were doing wrong.

In the Garden of Eden, there was probably a bird with a face that resembled Joan Rivers (with all the plastic surgery stretching her beak much too tightly) laughing about the fact that the leaf Eve was wearing was "so last season."

Writing the Declaration of Independence probably took longer than it should have because of Benjamin Franklin and his sense of humor. Thank goodness they vetoed his idea of the "right to life, liberty, and pursuit of whoopee cushions." And when he tried to add the joke about "arming bears" to the Constitution, the other delegates finally realized that Franklin was drinking again.

Can you imagine the short jokes that comics were doing during Napoleon's time? That was probably the time the term "French fry" cropped up.

And I'm sure that in The Battle of the Little Bighorn in 1876, one of Custer's guys was a comic who got in the last line of "Just a little off the top…"

Also in 1876, Bell invented the telephone. By 1877 comics had coined the phrase, "Do you have Prince Albert in a can?"

In 1888, Kodak started the craze of amateur photography. By 1889, comics were being arrested for cutting off people's heads to take funny pictures of them on top of other people's bodies. In their defense, this was pre-Photoshop. Also, we never said these were smart comics.

And so, I am just following the great comics of history as I say that I am running away to laugh at the world for a while. You'll find me in a comedy club somewhere with a rubber chicken, a pair of schnocker glasses, and a copy of my resumé. One of those is really hilarious. And the chicken and glasses are fun too.

Don't forget to tip your waitress…

> She changed her mind, but it didn't work any better than the old one.
> -Henny Youngman

Chapter 26

A "Finer Than Frog Hair" Gentleman

I'd like you to meet my father-in-law, Charles Elmo Atwood, also known as "Podie" as well as a number of other names which are unfit to print.

When I was younger, I went home crying because I didn't know how to handle his unorthodox sense of humor. Then I hit thirty and realized the man knew some stuff. When I hit forty, I realized this man is a genius. Let me explain by telling you some of his favorite expressions.

When asked how he is, he answers "finer 'n frog hair." On a really good day, it's "finer 'n frog hair split four ways."

Continuing on the hair theme, he likes to comment on my new haircuts with the saying, "I've seen better looking hair on salt meat."

When I proudly announced that I lost four pounds, he stood behind me and declared, "I found 'em!"

He lost his leg and his son in one awful week and still stands taller than anyone I've ever known.

After he lost his leg, he changed how he answers the question, "How tall are you?" He now answers, "Which side?"

When a nurse is silly enough to come near to put in an IV, he asks, "Does it matter which arm it goes in?" Of course, the helpful nurse says, "No." And he answers, "Then put it in yours."

He loves watching wrestling on television. He says, just because you know how it's going to come out doesn't make it any less entertaining. After all, he enjoys war movies and he knows how they end.

We like to watch *Deal or No Deal*. However, it's a different game for us. We look at all the young models on there and play our own game of "Real or Not Real." You figure it out.

He loves having me as his daughter-in-law. As he explains, "Some people got cancer. Some got diabetes. I got you."

When I accidentally took out a mailbox with my car, he wrote a lovely poem to commemorate the incident called, "The Lonely Sentinel." Nice to know I inspire him so.

He loves simple and old jokes. For example: A horse walked into a bar. The bartender looked at him and said, "Why the long face?" (Well, that's the only clean one I can remember.)

I love his stories of working on the railroad. He's still lightened by the memories of the friends he traveled with and weighed down by the collisions he survived.

He doesn't go into a building for his religion. He carries it with him everywhere he goes. He believes in treating other people decently, taking care of his family, and learning from the things that go wrong. Pretty simple stuff and pretty effective in creating a good life for those he comes in contact with.

He's fighting a battle in the hospital at the time of this writing and I've promised him $10 if he'll regain consciousness by tomorrow. I know he'll come out of it now. He'd never pass up a chance to take cash from me. Best ten bucks I'll ever spend...

Dad Atwood passed shortly after this column appeared in a magazine. This became part of his eulogy.

※★✶✳✶✦✱※
Don't cry because it's over.
Smile because it happened.
-Dr. Seuss

✺ ★ ✶ ✹ ✳ ⬢ ✳ ✺
I never leaf through a copy of
National Geographic without realizing
how lucky we are to live in a society
where it is traditional to wear clothes.
-Erma Bombeck

A-PARENT INSANITY

This section reminds us that parents and children have a special relationship.

That relationship is built on spending half a life trying not to be like the other one, half trying to be like the other, and the other half not sure what the hell we are trying to do because three halves just doesn't work.

Does this section apply to you? Answer the following questions:

- Have you ever said, "In my day…?"
- Do you worry when you think of kids today as your primary care provider of tomorrow?
- Do you believe that people become parents for one of three reasons:
    1. To be able to say, "I told you so."
    2. To have someone mow the lawn.
    3. Poor business hours at the local drugstore.

If you are breathing, this section is for you…

Chapter 27

THE SUNDAY AFTERNOON "WILL CHEAT FOR CHIPS" POKER CLUB

On Sunday afternoons, an elite club meets.

It consists of my 97 year-old father, my 39 year-old mother (dog years), my husband (ageless), and myself (do the math at your own peril).

This club is the Sunday Afternoon "Will Cheat for Chips" Poker Club. Each meeting starts the same way. Daddy tries to explain the rules of poker to Mom and me once again.

And, once again, Mom and I will ignore those rules. After all, we know that we have two perfectly good poker hands taped under our sides of the table to be used whenever things seem too hopeless. Unfortunately those hands are from a different deck and quite obvious due to the cartoon illustrations on them. Daddy tends to ignore this fact for us.

David tends to smile and nod a lot. It's a talent he's perfected over twenty-something years of marriage.

The games usually go something like this.

Mom insists, "This is ridiculous. Who dealt this terrible hand?"

I respond, "Let me think. Oh yes, it was you." I've never been known to be a kind child.

Mom ignores me. A talent she's perfected over sixty some-odd years of motherhood. (Very, very odd years.) "Well, I'll bet a red chip."

David looks dubious. "Twenty five dollars on a terrible hand?"

Mom responds quickly, "Don't worry. You're not in the will anyway." For a woman wearing a fake sunflower on her head, she's pretty quick with those kinds of responses.

As you notice during all of this, Daddy has been very quiet. That's because he's the only one at the table who really knows how to play this game. He's studying his hand while we're arguing over cards, the room temperature, and whose turn it is to go get pretzels.

We go through a few rounds of betting, which is a farce since Mom and I just bet color combinations, not actual denominations. We like patriotic hands with red, white, and blue chips. We tend to run out of chips pretty quickly.

Finally, bored with the slow pace of play, we move on to our Dr. Pepper round. This is where tens, twos and fours are all wild cards.

You've never lived until you've seen a poker game where four hands are laid down and are: five aces, a royal flush, five more aces, and six kings. (Mom sometimes refuses to give up all her cards when she draws new ones. She feels it is a communist plot if she has to give up a king.)

Yes, we've realized at the end of our game that we've solved no world problems. We've not decided what color we're going to paint the living room, which was our first discussion of the day. We haven't even decided who will get up to go get the pretzels. And that's my definition of a really good day.

※★*※*●*※
I could tell my parents hated me.
My bath toys were a toaster and a radio.
-Rodney Dangerfield

Chapter 28

ELDERLY WOMAN THWARTS WOULD-BE PURSE SNATCHER

The above headline in the online version of my hometown newspaper didn't even catch my eye. "Elderly Woman Thwarts Would-Be Purse Snatcher." Why should I look twice?

I should have.

That "elderly woman" was my mother. During our daily phone conversation she happened to mention that a young man had tried to relieve her of her purse that morning. I was stunned.

"Why didn't you tell me?" I screeched.

"I'm telling you now," she answered. She had a point.

"Okay, start from the beginning." As soon as I said those words, I realized my mistake. I was lucky she didn't go back to the Book of Genesis.

By the time she got to the point of the story where she was in the supermarket parking lot, I had dozed off three times.

"I had my purse in my shopping cart. I turned to unlock the car door and at that moment a young man drove right up next to my basket and reached out of his car to grab my purse. He pulled it right into his car."

I was wide-awake now. "What did you do?"

"I said, 'You're taking my purse!'"

"Good thinking, Mom. Otherwise he might not have realized he was robbing you."

"Don't be smart. It doesn't become you."

"Neither does having my 'elderly' mother attacked by a robber."

"I was never attacked," she corrected. "Now stop interrupting."

"Yes, ma'am."

"Well, he was a lovely young boy. Blond hair. Blue eyes."

"Thank goodness. I'd hate for you to be robbed by a person who would have an ugly mugshot."

Mom just cleared her throat. I understood. Be quiet.

"He had my purse in his hand and was putting the car in gear to leave when he smiled at me. Everything would have been okay if he hadn't smiled. That was just rude."

You know that at this point I wanted to interrupt. I was able to maintain silence, however I did bite my pencil in two in the process.

"So, when that little upstart smiled, I threw myself into the front window of his car, grabbed my purse, and yanked it out. He held the strap for a minute, and then I guess he realized I wasn't letting go. He let go of the purse and drove off."

"May I speak now?"

"I suppose."

In Celebration of Elastic Waistbands

"Are you insane?" I squealed. "You could have been killed. Was anything in that purse worth your life?"

"Actually nothing in the purse was important at all. It was the smile that made me do it."

I groaned. "Did they catch him?"

"Yes. I'm going to request that his sentence be spent working in my yard. After all, he was cute and he seemed pretty healthy."

I could just imagine the news story. "Elderly Woman Charged With Cruel and Unusual Punishment. Forces young man to listen to her stories about walking to school barefooted and her complaints about her children. Film at eleven."

But then again, he'll think twice before he turns to crime again...

My mother.
I wouldn't change a hair on her lip.

Chapter 29

THROW MAMA FROM THE BRIDGE

I am scared.

My mother and I are about to go on a book promotion tour.

Yes, I'm taking my mother on the road with me. This is the woman who taught me things like, "If you're not sure if a shirt is clean, sniff it. If your eyes don't water, it's clean."

The woman who plays poker by putting all her cards down and asking Daddy, "Did I win this time?" Usually she has a royal flush.

The woman who will take the opposite side in any debate just for a good fight, even if the debate is over whether baby seals should be clubbed or not.

The woman I played hide and seek with and she never found me. In fact, I suspect she never even looked.

In Celebration of Elastic Waistbands

The woman I am just like.

And all I can say is, *"Kill me. Please kill me."*

It seemed like a great idea at the time. We'll go on tour. Mom will sit quietly and demurely at a nice little table with me while I ask people to buy copies of my book. But, like all great ideas, it turned into something horrifying like those epilator things that "remove" hair from the roots. And now, here I am with the newly christened "Run Away From This Table" Book Tour.

Mother has decided to wear dark glasses and hold a cup emblazoned with the words, "Buy my daughter's book so I can eat." She plans to wear slippers and a robe so she can save on time getting ready for the events. And she wants to tell everyone the story of how I sucked my thumb until 4th grade. (Okay, really I think it was 6th, but I'm not going to admit that.)

The tour has changed from a short drive to a few markets around the state to a country-wide tour, during which time I will be trapped in various forms of public transport with a woman who once said that "If God had wanted us to make food from scratch, he wouldn't have invented Chef Boyardee."

It has turned into a nightmare where I will be forced to hear the story over and over again of how she didn't want a 6th child (guess which one I am) but she couldn't put me up for adoption because the other five wanted a puppy and she figured I would be easier to paper-train.

And, mere minutes ago she called me back with her new and improved slogan that's she putting on a sign to promote the book. "Buy this bad book. Otherwise you'll just waste the money on something silly like food."

I have chosen to spend time traveling with this 80-something-year-old rejectee from the Emily Post School of Etiquette. I think one of us is getting senile ... You decide which one...

Lassez le stratagème temps roulez...

⁂ ★ ✶ ✳ ✶ ✦ ✳ ⁂

I ask people why they have deer heads on their walls. They always say because it's such a beautiful animal. There you go. I think my mother is attractive, but I have photographs of her.

-Ellen DeGeneres

Chapter 30

STARTING THE NEXT NINETY-SEVEN YEARS

Today I'd like to introduce you to a remarkable person. Meet James Anthony Gabour, a man who celebrated his 97th birthday this year.

No, he didn't make a big deal about it. He didn't even take off work. After all, he reasoned, his grandfather didn't take off work for his 104th birthday, so why should he?

Yes, this is a special person. He doesn't brag about the fact that he is one of the last printers in the United States using a Linotype and melting huge bars of hot lead to mold into letters in his print shop. And he won't tell many of his stories that range from spotting enemy planes in World War II to teaming up with his wife to buy a weekly newspaper when the most he knew about running a paper was that it was printed on newsprint.

No, if you ask him about his big accomplishments, he'll just laugh and mumble something about a wonderful wife and six children, and being blessed. He won't tell you, but I'm his baby daughter, so I will…

This is a man who, during World War II, was a cook in the army. One time, a general came in after regular meal hours and asked nicely if Jim could fix him something to eat. Meeting someone nice enough to ask instead of order was a rare thing, so he was thrilled to fix one of the best breakfasts the man had ever eaten. I know, I've been eating those breakfasts for years and they're fit for a king … or even a president. Good thing, since that general was named Eisenhower.

A sense of humor is a necessary ingredient to life, he notes. For example, I recently got a letter from him. It was a single typed sheet that read, "I'm lost… I've gone to look for myself. If I should return before I get back, please ask me to wait. Dad."

This is a man who laughs when you mention retirement. "What would I do?" he jokes. So, instead he goes to Gabour Printing Company everyday and at lunchtime heads to the senior citizen center to help serve lunch to the elderly – all of whom are younger than he. In the evenings he heads out to visit his friends in the nursing homes. He feeds all strays, whether four-legged or two-legged. He can fix virtually anything, from machinery to skinned knees. And he loves to talk to people -- like a while back when a salesman, having no idea of Dad's age, tried to sell him some sort of twenty-year insurance policy. He just grinned and said, "Son, I'm an optimistic person, but that's just pushing it."

So, Jim, his ancient cat, his 39 year-old wife (trust him, don't argue with her about that), and his family celebrated 97 years of his making the world a better place this year.

And me – I love these birthday parties. He usually cooks some Lebanese food and tells some great jokes I can steal.

And the whole time, I'm praying that I've inherited not only that man's genes, but also his attitude...

When I was a boy the Dead Sea was only sick.
-George Burns

Chapter 31

MY MOTHER'S IN MY MIRROR...

I have been talking and listening at a lot of seminars lately and I'm finding a recurring theme.

We women are most afraid of one thing -- turning into our mothers.

The stories are endless...

"I searched for my glasses for twenty minutes yesterday," one woman told me.

"Well, we all do that," I comforted her.

"They were on my face."

I barely controlled the laughter ... and didn't bother to admit I had been looking for my reading glasses the day before when they were on top of my head.

The next story started with, "I saw my mom shopping with me yesterday."

"You saw her?" I was confused.

"It was actually my reflection in the mirror of the dressing room."

I nodded. Been there, done that, bought the elastic waist pants.

Another woman jumped into the conversation. "I told my daughter that I hoped someday she had a daughter just like her so she could see what she had put me through."

I nodded. "And this was prompted by…"

"A pierced belly button."

"And this same speech from your mom was prompted by …"

"Wearing makeup when I was sixteen," she laughed.

From others in the group, I heard amens.

"Mine came from wanting to wear a mini skirt."

"Mine was for sneaking out to see *The Exorcist*."

"Mine was because I made a C."

I smiled. Apparently voodoo dolls had no curse as strong as this threat of a mother…

Another woman came forward. "I have my mom's purse now. It's the size of carry-on luggage."

Everyone nodded at that one.

I agreed with that, but how can we help it? We were all raised on the show, *Let's Make a Deal*. We were waiting for Monty Hall to approach us and tell us that if we could pull a food processor out of our purse, we would win $100 or what was behind Door Number Three.

Another woman offered, "My mother insisted on turning leftovers into at least three other meals, none of which were recognizable."

I, too, remembered Beef Stew Hash-a-Roni.

Yet another comment: "My mom never gave me the talk."

Squeals of laughter came from the group.

"What talk? My mom told me on my wedding night that 'I'd know what to do'."

"Wow, that was a long talk compared to mine. Mom said, 'You went to a public school. I'm sure you read about it in the girls' restroom...'"

Another chimed in, "My mother said that you had to look out for boys. They were only out for one thing."

"Yeah, a housekeeper." This from the lady in the group who was on her third housekeeping job.

Then, a petite silver-haired woman on the back row smiled and spoke softly, "My mother taught me that I could be anything I wanted to be."

We all glowed. Other examples began to flow from all sides of the room.

"Mine showed me that anyone who said it was a 'man's world' had never watched a mother kiss a bobo and magically make it better."

"My mother taught me that you don't have to be the one in control to make things happen."

"My mom made me see that trusting myself was the first step of any journey."

I had to agree with all of the above. My mother made me realize that there is nothing stronger than a mother's hug when you're scared, nothing softer than a mother's kiss on a sleeping child's forehead, and nothing more loving than a mother's reprimand.

And so, if we think we are turning into our mothers, we are damn lucky...

A woman is like a tea bag.
You never know how strong she is
until she gets in hot water.
-Eleanor Roosevelt

HIT AND MISCOMMUNICATION

This section relates the stories of what can happen when we think we have communicated, but in fact have been talking to a person who is mentally vacationing on a beach in Biloxi.

We talk.

We pretend to listen while making grocery lists in our heads.

We use two dollar words to hide the fact that we're not certain enough of what we're talking about to use the clearer nickel word.

The challenge is that we've gotten so good at multi-tasking that we don't realize it's not appropriate when trying to really communicate with another person. Much like cleaning out your car's glove compartment is not a good idea when negotiating a lane change on a major interstate. (Don't ask.)

George Bernard Shaw had it right when he said that the problem with communication is the illusion that it has taken place.

Does this section apply to you? Answer the following questions:

- Do you think that communication with tin cans was more effective than cell phones?
- Have you ever listened to someone speak for an hour and answer, "Huh?"

If you got bored and skipped to the end of this list of questions, this section is for you...

Chapter 32

And, On The Eighth Day, A Committee Created The Camel

The old joke that a camel is a horse created by a committee is the most honest story ever written.

So many times, I have heard the words, "Let's have a committee look into that," and I always know what it means.

It is translated, "I haven't got a clue what to do. Let's put it off."

I have tried to make decision-making easier in so many ways. I have broken it down into twelve steps, crunched it into pro and con lists, tried the college football BCS method to computerize it, and balanced it with two sides of a coin.

The one thing that's always true is that eventually somebody has to finally make the decision.

It's not fun. Because if the musical chairs get pulled out and I'm the one left standing, I have to make the call. And that's when mistakes can happen. As long as I don't make a decision, I can't do anything wrong.

But I also can't do anything.

I always have to remind myself of the theme of my life, "I learn more from the wrong decisions than the right ones." In fact, today I'll go a step further and say that there are no wrong decisions. Just decisions I wouldn't make the same way again.

One day at a staff meeting it all came together for me...

"I have made a decision," I announced.

My staff looked confused. They have never before heard such bold words from me. "What is it?"

"We're going to try something new."

"New?" The girl at the far end of the table rolled the word around on her tongue as if it were the French word for kitty litter.

"Yes. We're going to take a chance. We're not going to do things the same old way that we've always done. And if things go wrong, I'll take the blame."

There were shocked gasps, raised eyebrows, and a burp from one corner of the table. I don't think my statement was actually responsible for the burp, but I'll take responsibility for the gasps and eyebrows.

I tore the paper in my hand and let the pieces flutter to the floor. More gasps. No burps.

"But we've always used that," the production fellow whispered.

"Not any more," I boldly stated.

"It might not work right," ventured the girl from legal. "It could be disaster."

"I don't care. Because sometimes a person has to take a chance. Where would we be if Christopher Columbus hadn't taken a chance?"

"What chance?" the girl from accounting shrugged. "He was using someone else's money for the trip."

"Yes, but what if he hadn't risked someone else's money? Where would we be today?"

"Spain?"

"You're not taking this seriously. What if Ford hadn't started that assembly line thing?"

"Car emissions wouldn't be messing up the planet?"

And it was then that I had my "ah-ha" moment. I realized that no decision is right. No decision is wrong. They just create a different path. And no path is good or bad. They're just different.

Suddenly, it took all the pressure off of me. I smiled and held up a paper to replace the one I had torn to shreds. Yes, I had made a decision.

"Italian instead of Chinese for lunch today!"

★ ★ ★ ★ ★ ★ ★

I'm considering cleaning the cabinet under my sink. I believe there's a possibility I will find Mr. Hoffa.

Chapter 33

DON'T TRY THIS AT HOME

There's an activity I like to do in some of my workshops.

This lesson in communication is a simple one that demonstrates the importance of all the parts of our messages. We take a sentence and discover how it can be changed without any changes in wording.

For example, we'll look at this statement: *I didn't say you looked stupid.*

A simple statement. Pretty straightforward. But let's play for a minute. Let's practice stressing different words in this same sentence.

Read the sentence with the emphasis on the underlined word.

<u>I</u> didn't say you looked stupid.
Translation: I didn't say you looked stupid, but I'm pretty sure that guy over there did. And he used some phrase about 'junk in the trunk.' He had a lot of other stuff to say too, but I won't go into all of it because you're already on your way to beat him up, so there's no need for me to continue.

I didn't <u>say</u> you looked stupid.
Translation: I didn't say it, but okay, let's be honest here. I was thinking it. That's much better, right? At least if I didn't say it out loud, you can hold onto that shadow of the doubt. I mean that look on my face might have to do with the fact that I discovered at lunch that tofu should not be used in tacos.

I didn't say <u>you</u> looked stupid.
Translation: I didn't say that you were the person who looked stupid. I was talking about that person standing next to you. Of course I wouldn't say that to him because he's got a tattoo that says "People-Person Hater" and seems to have a low tolerance level by the fact that he just beat up the coffee maker for smirking at him.

I didn't say you <u>looked</u> stupid.
Translation: You don't look stupid. You *are* stupid. Or maybe you're that guy in the previous example. Worse yet, you're the coffee maker that smirked at him.

I didn't say you looked <u>stupid</u>.
Translation: I really didn't say you looked stupid. I said you looked ugly. There's a huge difference. Of course, you might not appreciate either one, but I want to be sure you know how I'm insulting you because I'm a precise sort of person.

What do we learn from this activity?

Actually there are a number of morals to this lesson. You choose the one that most nearly suits your needs.

1. If written in print, we'll do almost any activity someone tells us to do. This explains some of our previous elections.
2. If you did this exercise out loud, you learned that the person in the cubicle next to you has the previously mentioned low tolerance level and a poor understanding of self-improvement exercises.
3. It's not what you say, but how you say it. Or how quickly you run after you say it.

There are two rules for success:
1) Never tell everything you know...
 -Roger H. Lincoln

Chapter 34

WORKING WITH CUSTOMERS... OR HOLDING A CARDBOARD SIGN BY I-10

Customers.

People complain about them more than any other single element of business. And yet, without them, we'd all be standing by the interstate with a cardboard sign.

I try to get this across to people when I teach seminars about customer service.

"If it weren't for the problems we encounter with our customers, they could have a machine do what we do," I suggest.

"Yeah," one person nods, "and they probably will soon."

"Oh no," I disagree. "Machines can never do what we do."

And for a moment I drift into a daydream. I'm on a phone call to my insurance company.

"You people have messed up my billing for the second month in a row," I insist through clenched teeth.

"Yes. I am the CSR3000. I will be working with you today," the machine replies.

"You're a machine?" I am surprised.

"Yes."

"Well, machine, I'm furious."

"Yes."

"I can't believe your company is so stupid."

"Yes."

Nothing more. The machine just says, "Yes."

"This is absolutely unacceptable," I growl.

"Yes."

"What are you doing, machine? You just keep saying yes."

"Yes. This is the portion of the call where I am programmed to allow the customer to vent. All I do at this time is to respond 'yes' until the customer has gotten his or her anger out of his or her system."

"Oh. What's next?" I am curious.

"Next I will apologize."

"That's ridiculous."

"I'm sorry."

Well, CSR3000 had just sneaked that step in on me. "Okay machine, what's next?"

"Next I am programmed to ask for details."

"You mean like the fact that your company billed me too late, and I didn't even receive the invoice until after the date the payment was due?"

"Thank you."

Well, we slipped past that portion quickly. "So machine, what's next?"

"I fix the problem." I hear a slight whirring sound and the clicking of keys. "I have submitted a revised mailing order and due date for you. It will work now."

I am intrigued. "Pretty impressive, CSR 3000. What do we do next?"

The machine doesn't miss a beat. "I apologize again and ask if you are satisfied with this solution."

"Interesting. And if I'm not satisfied?"

"I send an electrical shock through the phone line."

"I'm satisfied," I hasten to assure the machine. "Is that all there is to it?"

"Yes."

"It's interesting when you remove all the emotion from a problem, isn't it? Maybe we really do need machines to do customer service," I mused.

"Yes. Have a good day." The machine hung up.

It was strange, though. As the connection was broken, I could have sworn I heard a giggle.

Never let formal education get in the way of your learning.

-Mark Twain

Chapter 35

THE FIVE QUESTIONS YOU SHOULD NEVER ANSWER

I know that, in this day and age of copyright worries, everyone tells you not to copy things you see in magazines or books.

Today I'm telling you the opposite.

Copy this. Post it on your bulletin board at work. Mail it to friends. Have it tattooed on your pet. Because this is the list of questions that we need to circulate. We need to remove these questions from the face of the earth. They are dangerous and must never be answered.

Have I emphasized the importance of this enough?

Good. Then let me begin…

What are you doing Saturday?
No good can come of the answer to this question. It invariably means that this person wants you to do something on Saturday that you would not immediately agree to, or they would tell you what it was when they asked. They would say, "Do you want to come to a crawfish boil on Saturday?" Chances are you would answer "yes" to something like that. So, if they aren't telling you the activity, it is quite possibly something like, "Want to come over and work in my compost pile on Saturday?" This question is even more dangerous if you own a pickup truck, when the real question always involves the moving of heavy articles from one site to another.

How old do you think I am?
This question is always asked by people who believe they look younger than they are. If you answer wrongly, your relationship with this person is endangered. Even guessing a decade younger than you think they are doesn't work, because invariably they think they look two decades younger than that. Avoid this question by saying something noncommittal like, "Oh my gosh, I think that kangaroo is on fire!" If you are outside Australia, you can use variations on this theme.

Do I look fat in this?
You should pretend not to speak English if asked this question. Under no condition should you ever answer "yes." If you're forced into answering, under no condition should you hesitate even slightly before saying "no," And under no condition should you answer truthfully even if it is a white spandex dress on a woman in her ninth month.

Don't you just love (insert current music sensation here)?
People will never agree on musical tastes. And it does absolutely no good to lecture a person on the kind of music they should like. It is likewise the case for people who thought that *Citizen Kane* was the best movie ever made, who believed that *The Office* was a good way to train for the workplace, and who think that baby showers are fun. Thus, when someone asks for an opinion on something they obviously like such as Michael Bolton, it's in the interest of world harmony to say, "My, he does sing, doesn't he?"

What were you thinking?
This person obviously thinks you weren't thinking, so it's pretty useless to go on with this charade. The proper answer to this question is, "I was considering my place in the universe." It avoids answering the question, and it confuses them just long enough for you to sprint out of conversation range.

There they are. The five most deadly questions. With this list, I hope that I have done my part to make the world a safer place for us all. And now all I can say is, "Don't you think this was brilliant writing?" (Oops. Question Number 6.)

✯ ★ ✷ ✳ ✴ ✦ ✴ ✯

If you can't be a good example, then you'll just have to serve as a horrible warning.
                                              - Catherine Aird

Chapter 36

I GOT THE MOST POINTS... IN GOLF

And under the heading of "things that sound better than they really are," I actually had a chance to play in a golf tournament.

You might surmise that I actually know something about the sport, but after one hole of watching, you would know differently.

Understand that in this tournament, the number of us who actually knew which end of the club is used to hit the ball was less than the number of planets (minus Pluto, the now non-planet).

They were kind and allowed us to play "Best Ball". I don't know if that's a real way of playing golf or just something they made up to keep us from being embarrassed, but it basically meant that we all got to move our balls up to the site of the ball that went the furthest of our team.

After I spent the first ten minutes digging a small moat around my tee, I realized that "Best Ball" is great for new golfers who want to time their tournament by the clock and not the calendar.

I learned so much from the game, like the fact that members of golf clubs prefer that you stay within your assigned playing area rather than hitting across into the next green. (In my defense, I have the same problem with bowling alleys.)

It's a great sport to help with math skills as you determine how much sand is needed to fill the holes you make. It's great for negotiation skills as you try to talk the others on your team into letting you calculate your score in dog years. And I was thrilled to find that putting is not nearly as hard when you don't have to go through a windmill or a clown's mouth.

I made it out alive. However, it's funny how people get such different lessons out of an experience like that. A week later I ran into a friend from the tourney and we were discussing the event. He brought up what an incredible bonding experience it had been.

It seems that his team came together and, when some of them would start to have problems, a different person would always step up to lead as "Best Ball" person. He talked about the ways they kept each other enthused and how they worked together to pull a victory out of a sport that few of them had ever played.

My team learned lots of things too. We learned about sunburn. We learned that a golf club making contact with your ankle can cause words that make the Human Resources person on your team cringe. And I learned, after cheering wildly and receiving my "Bogey Award" trophy, that "getting the most points" is not as good a thing in golf as it is in baseball...

I dedicate this column with my apologies to the other members of my team and hope they all recover soon.

Baseball is 90 percent mental.
The other half is physical.
                    -Yogi Berra

DOMESTIC VIOLETS

This section addresses the never-ending battle of domesticity.

We were raised by the generation that still believed that a woman's place was in the home with a toilet brush surgically attached to the left hand and a ladle in the right, and the supreme hope that she kept her left and right hands correctly identified.

We believe that our homes should be ready at an instant for an inspection by Aunt Flo with her white gloves and solid black outfit that attracts pet hairs. And all of this should happen while we still make a living, keep a family in line with socially accepted morals (e.g., clothed), and a basic understanding of what's going on in the Middle East or Midwest or wherever things are "going on."

It's unrealistic. So this section is dedicated to those of us who have never had the desire to eat off our kitchen floors, who don't think it's such a bad idea to have the family eat over the sink, and whose idea of "housekeeping" is just paying the bills so we get to keep the house.

Does this section apply to you? Answer the following questions:

- Do you forget to do spring cleaning until August?
- Does your family think that pizza is one of the main food groups?

- Have you ever had to dust a pet who went under your bed?

If you ever have named a dust bunny, this section is for you…

✻ ★ ✦ ✳ ✶ ⬢ ✶ ✻

The most remarkable thing about my mother is that for thirty years she served the family nothing but leftovers. The original meal has never been found.

-Calvin Trillin

Chapter 37

MR. CLEAN GOES ON VACATION

Yesterday my mother came to visit.

This was amazing to me. I didn't realize pigs were flying these days. That, of course, was the prerequisite for her coming to visit me again.

The last time, after my cooking required the ceremonial removal of the battery from the smoke detector and mom recovered from the salmonella, I really didn't think she enjoyed the visit. But here she was, in ten short years, back to see me. So I must be doing something right.

Thus, being such an expert on domestic issues, I thought I would share with you a few household tips I have discovered.

- ❋ Cleaning your house without your glasses on makes the job go much more quickly.
- ❋ If you don't recognize something in Tupperware in your refrigerator, don't risk it.
- ❋ An electric toothbrush that has been overused is a great device for cleaning corners. Just remember not to accidentally put it back into the toothbrush holder.
- ❋ If you think your house is really dirty, don't clean it. Instead, go visit someone whom you know has a dirtier house than yours. Perspective is everything.
- ❋ Making your bed is a waste of time. You'll just have to do it again within 24 hours.
- ❋ Purchasing items with patterns that don't show dirt is a good rule for everything. I personally prefer dust-colored curtains, floors, and pets.
- ❋ "Don't try this at home" is a good rule to follow when watching chefs on television.
- ❋ If a commercial for a cleaning product has more than four disclaimers in small print, think twice.
- ❋ If God had meant for you to kill dust bunnies, he wouldn't have made your cats like them so much.
- ❋ There is a reason for the dimmer on light switches. Your lighting level should correlate inversely to the amount of dirt in your house.
- ❋ If we were supposed to throw all our old, broken junk away, architects wouldn't have invented hall closets.
- ❋ Once you find yourself considering rental of a storage shed as an additional closet, things have gotten out of hand.
- ❋ A bulldozer is not a bad idea for spring cleaning.

- ✻ If we cleaned all the time, spring cleaning would lose its thrill. And we can't have that, can we?
- ✻ No one has ever uttered the phrase, "Give me clean linoleum or give me death." So, it can't be all that important…
- ✻ If you can't remember if an item of clothing is clean or not, it is considered clean.

On a final note, why would anybody want to eat off the floor, anyway?

My second favorite household chore is ironing. My first being hitting my head on the top bunk bed until I faint.

-Erma Bombeck

Chapter 38

LOSING FOUND TIME

Sometimes it's a little embarrassing to realize that you've totally missed the point of a new discovery.

I realized this as I play with my favorite birthday gift to myself – my vacuuming robot.

Yes, I was drinking wine again while watching one of the television shopping networks. But this time I was actually sober enough to notice something useful. And when my new little friend appeared on my porch today, I realized that life would never be the same.

This incredible little toy looks like a stack of paper plates and runs around the house and vacuums while I do other things. The point of this is so that I don't have to waste time on silly things like cleaning floors, and instead I can work on books, client projects, family matters, and even paying household bills on time.

Now this all sounds quite grownup, doesn't it? And yet, here I sit on a Saturday morning, watching Hazel (I'm trying that name on for size) vacuum my living room. My husband comes in.

"A real timesaver, huh?"

"Absolutely!" I agree with relish. I'd agree with a hot dog too, but it's a little early in the day for that.

"So, what are you going to do now?"

"Oh, I just thought I'd keep Hazel company."

He is plussed. (I've always thought that if people can be nonplussed, they should be able to be plussed too.) "You do know that it's not alive, right?"

"Of course. But that doesn't mean she doesn't need company."

"Of course." Yeah, I know he's humoring me, but what do I care? I've got a robot vacuuming my house.

"So, you're not going to do anything else with this 'found' time?"

"I was thinking about having a Bloody Mary."

"That's all you're going to do with this free time?"

I nod. "You're right. That's just silly of me. I think I'll also have a Mimosa."

He shakes his head and retreats to the back of the house.

No, I don't really drink that much, but it's a great way to scare off a spouse who is acting like he has a great idea of something you could do with your spare time. If God had wanted me to clean that kitchen, he wouldn't have made old bread turn into penicillin.

Besides, right now I'm thinking of other uses for the robot. It's diverting my cats' attention away from forcing their way onto my lap while I try to type, so I'm thinking about attaching a tail to Hazel and see if I can get them to chase her around with dust cloths on their feet. That could double the use of the cleaning time.

For Halloween, I think Hazel is going to be a bat. The ears and wings will be so cute and she can carry the candy bowl on her back so I don't even have to stand up when kids come to the door.

And, the coup de grâce (or is it Coupe DeVille?) is that I can sit and watch Hazel and try to think of even more uses for her so I can avoid using my "found" time to address work, family, and bill-paying.

Now, if I can just teach her that I prefer two olives in my martini.

> ★ ★ ★ ★ ★ ● ★ ★
> Half our life is spent trying to find something to do with the time we have rushed through life trying to save.
> —Will Rogers

Chapter 39

CAT TOYS, HAIRBALLS, AND OTHER PURSUITS OF THE SUPERIOR SPECIES

My husband looked over and saw Shirley, my favorite sock puppet, crumpled on the floor.

"You never know what will end up being a cat toy, do you?"

I had to agree as I looked over at the toy pile for our animals. There was a pipe cleaner that had been attacked so many times that it had been shredded like old Christmas tree needles. Or were those actually Christmas tree needles from last year?

There was the poor maligned slipper that one of my cats had developed a romantic attachment to. A little unusual, but who am I to question a cat's lifestyle?

There was a copy of one of my books that the cats had dissected. Everybody's a damn critic these days.

And there was something strange. "What's that one?" I asked David as he leaned to get a closer look at it.

"Don't ask," he warned me, "but I think it's time for their hairball medicine again."

Yuck.

There was also a fuzzy mouse -- an actual cat toy that we had bought for our beasts. They've never touched that one.

There was a big round thing with a ball in it for them to chase around in a circle. They usually sleep on that.

There's a catnip-filled toy that has been felled and disemboweled like the proverbial wildebeest.

And, because cats have a sense of humor too, there was a pile of plastic dog poo.

"Can you tell me why our cats have dog poo in their toy pile?" David is curious.

"I believe that cats need a good laugh now and then."

"And you think they understand the concept of plastic poo?" He sees that our lovesick cat is now getting her head stuck in his slipper instead of playing with any of the toys.

"Of course. Cats have a great sense of humor. Why else would they get in their litter box and hang their bottom over the edge so they can miss the box completely?"

"Maybe they're slobs."

"Not our cats. Look at what gentlemanly manners Maddux has."

He looks at Maddux, our male cat, who is currently washing his unmentionables on the coffee table in front of us. "Yep, he's a regular Prime Minister candidate."

"And Poe is such a little lady."

He looks at Poe, who is currently launching herself at the unsuspecting Maddux. "Gentle as a lamb," he agrees.

We look at each other and smile as we once again hear the familiar sound of shredding coming from the eastern corner of our couch.

All we can think is "Thank goodness we didn't have kids."

My cat is smarter than I. If not, I'd be sitting on the couch scratching myself while the cat went off to work each day.

Chapter 40

TELEVISION, INTERNET . . . AND COLD TURKEY

Our cable and internet went out after one of our recent hurricanes.

Yes, both cable and internet. They were out for the whole week. It was hard to handle, but perhaps it was also good for me.

It was those first few minutes after the storm when I realized we had lost these services that were confusing. I stood, holding the remote control, moving closer and closer to the television – as if that would make it work.

But static remained on every channel I bounced past.

I had my sandwich with me, planning to eat it in front of a movie that I had only seen seven times. Without the television, I wasn't sure what to do.

"David, I need to eat."

He saw me holding my sandwich and the remote control. "The TV still isn't working."

"I know, but I can't decide where to eat. I always eat in front of the television. Is it against the rules to eat in front of it when it doesn't work?"

"Maybe not, but it does seem like there could be a better place."

We began searching through the house for a place to eat. We discovered a big surface in our dining area.

"What's that?" I pointed at the thing surrounded by chairs.

"I forgot about that. We have a dining room table," he smiled triumphantly. "That's where you're supposed to eat when you're not in front of the television.

"But isn't that where the cat sleeps?"

He looks at the tufts of hair on the glass top. "I think so. But we can clean it."

We both looked at each other and shared a hearty laugh.

I ate standing over the sink. But every day I would turn on the television and wait for some recognizable arm or leg to appear through the snow on the screen.

The withdrawal got worse when we realized we had no internet. We would turn on the computer and stare at the monitor.

"Does it do anything?" I questioned my technically-savvy husband as we surveyed the undersea picture and waited for something to happen.

"It holds those little figurines on top." He points proudly to a zebra, a pig, and Spongebob Squarepants.

We sat and stared at the screensaver for a while. And then I did something completely amazing. I read a book. Then another. Then another. I read everything in the house, including the instruction manual for my refrigerator. Did you know you're supposed to clean those things occasionally?

It was a long week. We solved the dining problem by eating out all week. To combat the internet withdrawal I would write cryptic notes to my husband with symbols like :) and terms like LOL and slip them under the door of his office and run away. We called it manual email.

Through the week, we found ourselves reading together in the evenings. We spent hours discussing the deep issues of the day. We played catch in the back yard, a new territory we had not known existed.

We spent an entire week away from the mindless flipping of channels and internet surfing. It was healthy. It was intellectual. And thank goodness, as soon as the cable guy came, it was over...

I read the fable of a man who moved a mountain with patience and a spoon.
All my life I've been waiting for someone to give me caffeine and a bulldozer.

Chapter 41

My Cat Is More Popular Than I

It's embarrassing to admit it, but my cat has a better social life, more business prospects, and a better credit rating than I have.

It all started a few months ago when I wanted to see who was selling my name to mailing lists. I began to sign up for information, register on websites, and enter contests in my cat's name. Maddux Atwood. It was enlightening.

It started when Maddux began receiving more junk mail and email than I've ever had. To date, he has been informed that he has won bunches of items, including a great vacation, a free diet plan, and last week, he won a PlayStation 2. Great prize for someone without opposable thumbs.

He might have already won the Publisher's Clearinghouse, but there are two other names on the list that

I think are probably smarter animals and so I encouraged him not to bother to send in his entry.

He was offered a great price on a laptop computer. However, realizing this might slow him down in his work each night, he decided to pass. His nighttime job is continually circling the interior of the house to ensure that no one sleeps longer than 17 minutes at a time.

Cruise lines are fighting over who can offer him the best price and upgrades on a Caribbean cruise. But, he has a thing against water, so he refuses to answer them. They just keep on sending better offers.

He began to get rather suggestive emails and some that were downright rude. They offered to show him things that a young tomcat his age should not be shown and even tried to sell him medications, especially Viagra. I wondered if I should write back to tell them that Maddux is neutered.

Then, apparently because he was receiving so many lewd offers, the email gods decided he needed salvation. A complimentary bible is now waiting in the name of Maddux Atwood.

He also apparently has a better credit score than I do. Happy little emails have come offering him ways to knock out his existing debt. He receives numerous mail offers for low percentage rates on credit cards. And, to add insult to injury, he's pre-approved. Me? I have to beg for extended credit.

He was offered membership in the National Geographic Society and right now is deciding if he wants to use his new Platinum Visa to get dish television. And BellSouth will not leave him alone.

It's a little hard to swallow. I have never won anything. My credit applications cause great giggling when people see the "self-employed" occupation. Yet he, an entremeower, can get pretty much anything he signs up for. I wonder if you can have discrimination on basis of species. I'd like to sue somebody over this.

And so, as I watched Maddux sitting on his latest copy of Reader's Digest, I decided he was getting too big for his britches. Or whatever cats wear. I showed him. Today my other cat, Poe Atwood, bought her first item on Ebay, an old William Powell black and white movie. Let the games begin...

There's no dealing with a cat
who knows you're awake.
                    -Brad Solomon

When dogs leap onto your bed,
it's because they adore being with you.
When cats leap onto your bed,
it's because they adore your bed.
                              -Alisha Everett

FAMILIES, CLUBS, CULTS... THE LEERY OF RELATIVITY

This section looks at some of the many groups we find ourselves attached to during the course of our lives, from family units to clubs, associations, and the occasional cult.

These connections happen because humans are social creatures. It is a genetic fact that a human being must tell at least twenty-seven knock-knock jokes in order to move on to the prepubescent stage of life. And that same human must send at least 2,277 email jokes during the midlife portion of life.

Thus the invention of clubs. It makes it easier to get mailing lists.

Does this section apply to you? Answer the following questions:

- Do you think there's another reason for the term "relative insanity?"
- Did you once go to the bathroom during a club meeting and come back to find you had been elected president?
- Do you realize that club and cult only differ by one letter?

If you have a family or have ever used caller ID to avoid being put on a bake sale committee, this section is for you...

Chapter 42

THE ATWOODS AND 2.5 CATS...

Every so often I like to send my family a newsletter to tell them I'm still alive, update them on my latest career, and ask for money.

Since I've been writing for so long now, I must admit that I feel like you brave readers are part of my family. After all, you're the ones who read my meanderings in the futile hope of finding something of value. (My suggestion there is to keep looking. It could happen someday.)

And now, you poor souls are on my newsletter list. So here it is...

Greetings from Atwood Manor ...

When last we left David and Christee, they were poor, struggling "entre-manures" with too many stray animals and too little sense. This year, things are really different. Now they are poor, struggling entre-manures with too many stray animals and absolutely no sense. Thank goodness for progress.

David is still doing voiceovers for lots of commercials. People across the United States hear his wonderful voice on radio and television saying deep, reassuring things like, "Licensed drivers only", "The lottery is now up to $38 million dollars" and "Tastes like chicken."

Christee is still doing anything short of dancing on tables to make a living. And, if they made a table strong enough to hold her up, well, who knows... Christee is now on a promotional tour for her book where she scares audiences across the country by standing outside bookstores and offering free bookmarks made of scrap paper to anyone who will slow down long enough to look at a copy.

Currently the Atwoods have 2.5 cats. Don't ask. The answer is not pretty. Which brings up the question, "Would any of you like a .5 cat?"

Christee continues her close relationship with Prozac. Yes, she got off of it for a while. Once again, the phrase "not pretty" comes to mind. (Note: Dark chocolate, even when fashioned into cute little capsules, should not be considered as a permanent substitute for antidepressants.)

David continues to ride his Harley and now insists on calling the car a "cage". Christee, dangerous enough on four wheels, and having terrorized both people and defenseless orange cones in a motorcycle driving class, has reverted to cruising on a bicycle with training wheels.

Christee has also moved back into the elastic end of her closet, which includes a far abridged selection of clothing. She basically chooses each day between wearing a striped dome tent or a brown vinyl boat cover. She's trying yet another diet, having received her annual welcome back invitation from the Big-Boned Chicks' Exercise Salon and Grill.

Life is good. It is interesting. And it is expensive. Send your donations now to the Atwoods' Pet Emancipation Fund. And, in homage to Dave Barry, wouldn't "Pet Emancipation Fund" be a great name for a rock band?

All our love,
Christee, David,
& assorted rodents

✦★✶✳✶✦✳✦

Happiness is having a large, loving, caring, close-knit family in another city.
 -George Burns

Chapter 43

ALL GROWN UP BUT NOT DEAD YET

I have discovered a new stage of life.

All our lives we've known about infancy, childhood, adolescence, and adulthood. We've heard terms like midlife and old age bandied about. But today I'd like to propose a new life stage.
It's called AGUNDY and it covers everything from age 25 to our second-to-last breath. It stands for "All Grown Up But Not Dead Yet."

- Agundyers are those of us who have reached the age where we should be adults, but we refuse to admit it. We are those people who refuse to pass the toy row in the grocery store without taking a look ... and occasionally pushing a child to the side as we gaze in adoration at the new rack of comic books ... oh, excuse me ... "graphic novels".

- Agundyers have a desire to kiss cashiers who ask for their IDs when buying alcohol.

- Agundyers still accidentally say, "I bought the new Aerosmith album" instead of "I bought the new Aerosmith CD."

- Agundyers have the buttons programmed on their car radio to adult stations, public radio, and even classic rock, but at one end there is a button for that station that plays window-rattling music.

- Agundyers get very tired of saying, "Yes," when they want to say, "Are you #$%^&* crazy?"

- Agundyers remember typewriters, carbon paper, and having to retype an entire page of their high school research paper because they forgot to leave space for the #$%^&* footnotes.

- Agundyers have an occasional desire to replace the phrase #$%^&* with the actual words.

- Agundyers remember when the response to a tan was, "Nice tan. Where have you been?" instead of "Nice tan. Bottle, booth, or airbrush?"

- Agundyers want the right to call in "sick and tired" to work. They occasionally slip and say "I don't wanna go to school today," when their alarm goes off in the morning.

- When someone says, "Act your age", Agundyers automatically want to revert to 19.

- Agundyers still sniff copied materials to see if they catch the scent of those purple mimeographed pages from school days.

- Agundyers have incredible eyesight. They can look in a mirror and see the 1974 version of themselves.

- Agundy females dream of going to slumber parties to do their nails, talk about boys, and watch reruns of *Dark Shadows* just to see the beleaguered Barnabas and Quentin with his massive sideburns.

- Agundy males dream of having an exclusive club like the Little Rascals used to have, "The He-Man Woman-Haters Club," where the courts won't insist that Agundy females can join.

- Agundyers are pretty good at breaking off their romantic relationships that aren't working out, but they still haven't figured out how to "break up" with obnoxious friends. (Definition of obnoxious: Any person who reminds me of me.)

- Agundyers often think how much faster it would be to say things nowadays if there were no such term as "politically correct."

And so, for today, I think I'll let my Agundy side have its way. When someone looks at me and says, "Isn't that outfit just a little too 'young' for you?" I think I'll answer, "Yes. Isn't it great?"

I think I can live with this AGUNDY thing...

★ ★ ★ ★ ★ ★ ★ ★

If God had wanted us to fly,
He would have given us tickets.
-Mel Brooks

Chapter 44

A Club Is Born, Dies, and Is Reincarnated

Every so often, I like to start new clubs. This is a ploy to keep me from doing any sort of meaningful work. This month's club is the Thirsty Thursday Drinking & Writing Club.

Based on our first meeting, we seemed more focused on the former than the latter.

The formal name of our group is BRAT, the Baton Rouge Algonquin Table. If you don't know about the Algonquin, look up Dorothy Parker and you'll discover it was a seedy little circle of literati who enjoyed getting together, drinking, and speaking poorly about anyone who didn't show up.

The invitation to BRAT included a warning against high expectations by noting that, "We will use this time to drink, be rude, and then sober up before we drive home. This group has no redeeming social value ... and if you happen to pick up some useful information during the course of the evening, it will be totally by accident."

In our first three minutes we discussed, in order: 1) the purpose of our meeting, 2) what drinks to order, 3) whether we should actually have a purpose to our meeting, 4) what drinks were included in happy hour, 5) whether we cared if there was a purpose to our meeting, 6) how many drinks we could order before happy hour ended, and 7) if any food should be included in our order. We then adjourned the meeting to hold the "after-meeting social."

It was the most productive non-meeting I've ever attended. We decided to resist any temptation to organize the group. The most organized we will get is to set future meeting sites. Requirements for meeting sites: the aforementioned drinks and happy hour prices.

The group has no officers, no mission, and absolutely no class. Our numbers include everything from the "in-transition" members to the gainfully employed to those who refuse to admit they are "in-transition" by putting the title, "Author", after their names. (Why does everyone always look at me when I say that?)

My initial plan was to include the discussions from the evening in this book so that they could be preserved for posterity when this new Algonquin moved into the pages of history. Upon comparing our discussions with the current code of decency, I determined that the only portion I could, in good conscience, include, was a discussion of how cold it was.

At the end of the meeting, unable to decide the location of our next gathering, we left promising we would get someone to make a decision before next month.

The meetings of BRAT, which has now officially morphed into the Thirsty Thursday Drinking & Writing

Club, are held occasionally at roving locations. In order to find out the location, you must send an email to someone who is a member. Your subject line must include "Need secret location" or it will go directly to a junk mail folder and be lost among hundreds of emails that promise all sorts of things that I believe to be physically impossible. And, if you know of a place to get secret decoder rings, please contact one of our members so that you can be made president of the group.

This chapter is offered with apologies to Amy, our waitress.

>Please accept my resignation.
>I don't want to belong to any club
>that will accept me as a member.
>   -Groucho Marx

Chapter 45

The "Doctor, It Hurts When I Do This" Association

I received another AARP invitation in the mail this week.

After beating my head against the refrigerator door for approximately 12.75 minutes, I opened it and grabbed cheesecake. This is, of course, the universal cure for melancholy.

Then I decided to embrace my oldness by connecting with others who have received this postal "badge of honor".

If you would like to be considered for membership in this totally unofficial association of chronologically-challenged citizens, please consider the following questions:

- Did you spend more on your mattress than on car accessories in the past year?

- Do you compare current events with television shows that no one in your office remembers? Example: "I think this happened on an episode of *Father Knows Best*."

- Ladies – Do you put more pads in your shoes than your bras?

- Men – Do you get a sunburn on top of your head?

- Do you have to fight the overwhelming desire to pull up a teenager's pants?

- Do you still want to root through your Mom's purse for change when you hear the ice cream truck?

- Have you ever considered driving to your mailbox?

- Do you still use phrases such as "a wild and crazy guy," "Where's the beef?" and "I can't believe I ate the whole thing?"

- Did your family grow up shopping on Double Green Stamps Tuesdays?

- Do you look forward to going home after long trips so you can use your own bathroom?

- Do you no longer care who sees you adjusting body parts and stray clothing straps?

- Do you count vacuuming as an aerobic workout?

- Do you know the next line of the jingle, "You can take Salem out of the country but…?"

- Do you remember the prefix word that came before your childhood phone number?

- ✳ Do you believe that no one should have more tattoos than they have nipples?
- ✳ Ladies – Do you watch NCIS for Ducky instead of the sexy young actors?
- ✳ Do you keep a handheld poker game in your bathroom?
- ✳ Do you look through your memory box and not remember?
- ✳ Do you remember thinking that Archie Bunker was cutting edge?
- ✳ Do you remember when you used to carry a nickel for the phone instead of carrying a phone?
- ✳ Has your idea of true success changed from being a millionaire to having a sound 401k?
- ✳ Do you have hangovers without drinking?
- ✳ Do you have to make sure that someone is nearby to help you up when you get an item off a lower shelf at the store?
- ✳ Have you ever pooped out on the third floor of your Stairmaster? Was that Stairmaster recently featured in a classified ad?

Congratulations! That person next to you, who is nodding as you read this list aloud, is really old.

✳ ★ ✶ ✽ ✶ ✤ ✽ ✳

I refuse to think of them as chin hairs.
I think of them as stray eyebrows.

—Janette Barber

Chapter 46

The Ack-ARP Card

Yes, I finally did it. I joined.

I received my AARP card in the mail. I went through all the stages of grief. Okay, I lied. I got stuck at denial.

It's not that it bothers me to age. The alternative would be a darn site inconvenient for my mortgage company, who is really counting on my loan payments.

The problem is that I am self-employed. Retirement is not an option. Oh sure, I could have one of those fancy retirement plans that gives me money in my old age, but that would mean giving up on the immediate gratification and luxuries that my current income allows me – namely electricity, groceries, and cat food (not necessarily listed in order of priority).

Planning for tomorrow just seems too un-Zen for me. I'm supposed to live in the moment. I'm supposed to be present in the here and now. I'm also supposed to have that cool device they showed on television that makes you lose weight without diet or exercise; just the use of well-placed shock treatments.

While all of these comments sound like excuses for a lack of future planning, I'd like you to know that they're not. They're justifications. Okay, here's another admission. I just used my thesaurus to find another word for excuse. Yup, they're excuses.

I guess the lesson here is that there's no excuse for lack of planning, but there's also no way to force someone to plan who refuses to grow up, much less accept growing older.

You can try to embarrass them into planning, but that only works if they're socially acceptable-type people. You've read enough of my chapter by now to realize that's not the situation here.

You can try to scare them with horror stories of their impending poverty, but most of us non-planners live in the "lottery is my retirement system" world where we're waiting for that one big "fix" that will save us from ourselves.

You can try to give incentives, but that didn't work for us even in the days when banks gave out toasters to people who started savings accounts.

Nope. These people have to make the decision themselves. They have to have an "ah-ha" moment that propels them into action. And mine was the receipt of that AARP card.

I decided that I would do research into programs that could help me during my retirement years. I bypassed IRAs and went straight into looking up the value of my body parts. After careful consideration, weighing the options, and reviewing all possible alternatives, I have made a decision.

No, it is not an intelligent one, but you knew better than to expect that from me, right?

I will not worry about tomorrow. I will not consider retirement. In fact, I will take up a new occupation at the age of 65.

Now, if I can just find a training class on shark dentistry.

> I've got all the money I'll ever need
> if I die by four o'clock this afternoon.
> —Henny Youngman

ATTITUDE ALTERCATIONS

This section looks at how some people get lemons and make lemonade and the rest of us have a tendency to throw those lemons at the people making a success with their lemonade stands.

    Attitude is the thing that separates artists from people with paint sets.

    Attitude changes a devastating blow to a temporary setback.

    Attitude is the thing that we try to change at happy hours, but more often we find ourselves ending up with a bad attitude and a hangover.

Does this section apply to you? Answer the following questions:

- Do you know that we carry our own weather?
- Do you know lots of people who carry tornadoes?

If you have ever used "sign language" on the interstate, this section is for you…

Chapter 47

ZEN AND THE ART OF NOTHING

My husband came into the living room the other day and there I sat, in the middle of the floor, with a big goofy grin on my face and a cat chewing on the laces of my Reeboks.

"I'm thinking that there's some special meaning to this," he began.

"You're so right," I nodded vigorously, sending the cat into another attack on the unsuspecting shoelace. "I found Zen!"

"And was it missing?"

"For me it was." I noticed him getting comfortable on the couch. He is accustomed to long speeches from me every time I have an "ah-ha" moment. "I'm in the moment."

"Good place to be," he nodded.

"But I've never really been 'in the moment' before. You see, when I used to meditate, I had to have complete silence or special music or one of my tapes talking me into relaxation. Today, I don't have that. Today, I'm meditating with my eyes open."

He looked closely. The cat had moved on from the shoelace and was working on giving me a gift of a hairball. The phone was ringing. In the distance the washer was buzzing, alerting me to a load of clothes that had gone off balance ten minutes prior. And I was still sitting in the middle of the floor, smiling that goofy "ah-ha" grin.

"You're definitely in the moment."

"I finally get it."

"And it is?"

"This moment is all there is. Whatever came before was just leading up to this moment. This ah-ha. Whatever comes after isn't here yet and so I can't control it. This is the moment. This is what I've been waiting for all my life. The moment that I couldn't wait for if I was truly living in the moment."

He nodded again. I kept going.

"It was fine that I could meditate when conditions were perfect. Now I can meditate when they're not. That's even more important."

"Good thing. Conditions are seldom perfect in a house with stray cats, pet termites, and only one Harley."

"I've learned to multi-task so well that I've forgotten it's not right for every aspect of life."

"I thought we realized that during your 'I can drive better when I'm cleaning the glove compartment' era."

"Obviously I hadn't learned it well enough. I realized it last week when I was meditating at the same time as watching television, hemming my pants, and cleaning the oven."

"Is that why there was a pair of pants in the oven?"

"Slight lapse in concentration. But that's not the point."

"And the point is?"

"All my life I've waited for the perfect moment. And, while waiting, a million perfect moments occurred. I just didn't notice them because I was too busy looking for them."

Strangely enough, he got it. And so did I.

He went outside to practice Zen and the art of motorcycle maintenance. I stayed inside and practiced Zen and the art of nothing. And we both were in very good moments.

My goal for today is to stop thinking
I'm God's intern ...

Chapter 48

HAPPILY EVER AFTER ... AFTER WHAT?

During the romantic month of February with Valentine's Day and the remorse that always follows the consumption of an entire heart-shaped box of chocolate in one sitting, I have this to say: Fairy tales did us a great injustice.

They always ended with ... "And they lived happily ever after." They never went a step further.

The fairy tale never went beyond that moment when beautiful Cinderella and handsome Prince Charming kissed at the altar. Never saw the time when Cinderella's sixteen-inch waist expanded and she had to resort to lots of elastic waistlines. Never got to the point where Prince Charming realized his receding hairline and bald spot were starting to meet and the shine was affecting family photographs.

And so, they never showed us true love.

Hey, it's easy to be in love with Snow White when she looks like a china doll. (Although those seven strange guys hanging around her should probably have worried her prince.)

And it's no problem to drool over Hercules as he flexed those muscles and tossed bad guys over his shoulders. (Yeah, he's not technically a fairy tale, but I like the actor Kevin Sorbo, so I had to mention that.)

But what happens when those hairs start graying and the waistline is hanging a little over the belt? Well, that's when true love steps in.

These are the times we should have seen in fairy tales. We should have seen how love prevailed when Cinderella's house-cleaning service failed and they lost their savings. We should have been exposed to the point where Prince Charming became a workaholic and had to go through counseling. We should have seen the period where the Prince drooled over his royal secretary who was 20 years younger than his bride.

But more importantly, we should have seen them live through these experiences and become stronger individuals within a stronger union.

True "Happily ever after" is ...

- Learning to like football because it means sharing Sunday afternoons with your prince.
- Listening to the pros and cons of a new hairstyle because your princess can't decide on her own.
- Ignoring the fact that the clothes hamper is a foreign land to your spouse.
- Learning that saying "You look fine" is very close to saying "You look like Roseanne at her largest."

- Understanding that "wanting space" is not a permanent condition.
- Realizing it's okay to compare in-laws to prehistoric creatures on the Discovery Channel. (Oops, how did that one get in there?)

Yes, true love is realizing that you love Prince Charming or Snow White not in spite of their warts and foibles (Do people still use the word foible?), but because of them. Because all those warts, past experiences, and changes over the years are what make our princes and princesses who they are today. And that's someone pretty special who we've grown with, changed with, laughed and cried with. And isn't that what living "happily ever after" is really all about?

✯ ★ ✦ ✳ ✶ ✽ ✶ ✯

Love at first sight is easy to understand;
it's when two people have been looking at each
other for a lifetime that it becomes a miracle.
-Sam Levenson

Chapter 49

BEING HAPPY RUINED MY LIFE

D arn.

I got the call today that every author dreams of. A nationally syndicated television show wanted to fly me out to talk about my midlife crisis.

It was my moment to shine. I was already practicing holding my breath to look skinnier and seeing if clear packing tape would hold up my extra chin long enough for the interview.

But then, in the phone pre-interview, the producer started asking me questions like, "What trauma made you realize how terrible midlife crisis is? Did your husband leave you?"

"What?"

He explained, "That's what we want to hear about. Overcoming trauma to get through a midlife crisis."

I was confused. "But if I think about it as trauma, then I probably haven't really overcome it."

He persisted, "But for the show we want to talk about the trials and tribulations, the problems of midlife."

"But I'm really happy. I like talking to other people and realizing that I'm not alone in this midlife crisis thing."

He was frustrated. "That's not what we're looking for."

"You mean if I'm not depressed I can't be on the show?"

"Well, it's not our focus to see midlife crisis as funny."

I thought for a moment. I could have run into the other room and asked my husband to leave me so I could be on the show. I considered it for a moment. A very long moment. After all, it is national television.

But then I thought about what I stand for. Yes, I've experienced the 3 Ds. Death, Disaster, and Dimpled thighs. I've also been depressed, flat broke, and had a bad hair decade.

And if I focused on those things, I could sound just as pitiful as any person who's ever cried their way through an episode of *Oprah*. But that's not how we elastic folks get through a crisis.

Maybe the national media needs to realize that the kind of survival that gets us through hurricanes, deaths of loved ones, and yes, even midlife, is the kind of survival that says, "You get through it, you move on, and after a respectful amount of time, you make fun of it." (Unless it's a president you don't like. Then you don't wait the respectful amount of time.)

So I'd like to share my email to the producer with you.

Darn!! Wish I focused on my traumas a little more so I could be on the show!!!

But I can't — that's the biggest emphasis of my midlife crisis. I have to find the humor in my trials and tribulations or I'd have gone crazy by now. Oh wait... I think that ship has already sailed... Never mind...

So, with a healthy sense of humor, a good supply of Prozac, and my fancy car that goes from zero to sixty in just under a weekend, I'm good to go for midlife.

Thanks for talking with me and please keep me in mind if you ever decide to do a show on "Using humor to laugh your way through midlife" ... or "How to embarrass yourself in six easy steps." I'm an expert on both of those...

So, yet again, I'm still one step away from the "big time" – and all because I'm contented.

I've never been so depressed about being happy.

The Constitution only guarantees the American people the right to pursue happiness. You have to catch it yourself.

-Benjamin Franklin

Chapter 50

TAKING A HUMOR INVENTORY

You know how sometimes nothing seems funny?

I find that this is the perfect time to slow down, put on a silly hat, and take a humor inventory.

A humor inventory is the process of reminding yourself of the stuff that's funny to you. Sort of a spelunking mission to rediscover your sense of humor. Here's how the process works for me.

First, I read the newspaper. No, not the depressing details – mainly the headlines, unusual stories, and ads. Or, if I'm really lazy, I just read other people's summaries of the newspapers. Or just the email joke versions of other people's summaries of the newspapers.

I find headlines that make me giggle like these:
- Blizzard Hits Four States. One is Missing.

- Lawyer to Offer Poor Free Advice
- Grandmother of eight makes hole in one
- Police begin campaign to run down jaywalkers
- Squad helps dog bite victim
- Two sisters reunite after eighteen years at checkout counter
- Something went wrong in jet crash, experts say

Advertising has its own brand of humor:
- Classified ad: Dog, faded brown, three legs, one ear missing, blind left eye, broken tail, recently neutered. Answers to the name Lucky.
- For sale: an antique desk suitable for lady with thick legs and large drawers.
- Dinner Special – Turkey $2.35; Chicken or Beef $2.25; Children $2.00.
- Now is your chance to have your ears pierced and get an extra pair to take home, too.
- We do not tear your clothing with machinery. We do it carefully by hand.
- Tired of cleaning yourself? Let me do it.
- Dog for sale: Eats anything and is fond of children.
- Stock up and save. Limit: one.
- Man, honest. Will take anything.
- Man wanted to work in dynamite factory. Must be willing to travel.
- A used car lot advertised: Why go elsewhere to be cheated? Come here first!

And now, the Superstore – unequaled in size, unmatched in variety, unrivaled inconvenience.

I often enjoy the acerbic humor of bumper stickers. It's the mailboxes I take out while reading them that I don't enjoy:

- As long as there are tests, there will be prayer in schools.
- I still miss my ex-husband, but my aim is getting better.
- My Hockey Mom can beat up your Soccer Mom
- If you can read this, I can slam on my brakes and sue you!
- Jesus is coming. Everybody look busy.

I also find examples of humor in unexpected places. Here are some statements supposedly taken from medical reports – and if an email says that, it must be true, right?

- By the time he was admitted, his rapid heart rate had stopped and he was feeling better.
- Patient has chest pain if she lies on her left side for over a year.
- On the second day the knee was better and on the third day it had completely disappeared.
- The patient is tearful and crying constantly. She also appears to be depressed.
- Discharge status: Alive, but without permission.

These are the sorts of things that jumpstart my sense of humor.

Well, these and a cheap box of wine. But these have fewer calories.

★ ★ ★ ★ ★ ★ ★ ★

When I'm in traffic jams, I do not get stressed. Instead I pretend I'm in a parade and wave at everyone.

Chapter 51

WHAT ELSE?

I caught the flu that had been going around.

I was so sick that I actually had to miss a meeting. For me, that's one of the signs of the apocalypse. I remember driving the porcelain bus thinking, "What else could go wrong?"

I hadn't completely recovered when a beloved member of my family passed away. Broken-hearted, we walked out of the door to go to the funeral home and the family dog got out. He ran toward the street, where a pit bull came dashing toward him. "What else?" I tried to yell, but it came out sounding more like another four-letter word.

I ran gallantly toward the dogs to break up the inevitable fight. Unfortunately, in my haste I had gained enough momentum so that I couldn't stop. I caught a heel on the side of the driveway, started spinning with all the grace of an NFL lineman performing *The Nutcracker,* and in slow motion found myself plummeting into a ditch. All the while a pair of amused dogs sat amiably side by side, watching.

With a cast on my broken hand I delivered the eulogy. Yes, you'd think this was a "What else?" moment, but I already knew what else. I had a book due to my publisher in two days.

Thus, I sat, pecking at keys with my left hand and two fingers on the right poking out of my cast, reaching blazing speeds of up to ten words per minute. My voice recognition software refused to translate my southern English correctly, so I'd "what elsed?" it right off my computer.

Then I realized I had a class to teach in the next week and it was on, of all things, "Attitude is Everything." Very much like having Lizzie Borden teach an anger management course. I was ready to yell a great big obscene "What else?" on that one, when the cat jumped on my computer and knocked half my equipment to the floor.

I sat on the floor near my wrecked equipment, ready to cry. Strangely enough I heard myself chuckle instead, especially after my other cat came to inspect the damage and deposited a hairball. Then, I heard the swoosh of letters dropping through the mail slot on my door. I looked and there was the bill for the x-rays of my hand.

I started laughing hysterically. My eyes leaked. My cats ran away. My mail carrier hurried off my porch. And I sat on the floor and guffawed until my ribs ached.

I grabbed my low-tech pen and paper and started to write my attitude class. Because now it all made sense.

Life is full of lumps. Some are small. Some are incredibly overwhelming. That will never change. The only thing that changes is my response to those lumps. I can sit and start linking them all together to create a depressing blanket that covers my life, or I can see them as they are – separate events that create a life truly lived. I can think that karma or the higher power is out to get me or I can realize that I am going through the same sorts of experiences that everyone has gone through since the beginning of time.

So my success in life is not wallowing in my "what elses?," but instead celebrating what else I can overcome to create a better me.

I'm ready for that attitude class now.

✯ ★ ✦ ✳ ✵ ◆ ✳ ✯

I learned in school that money isn''t everything.
It's happiness that counts.
So Momma sent me to a different school.
　　　　　　　　　　　　-Zsa Zsa Gabor

A WRITER'S LIFE: A DOG'S LIFE WITHOUT THAT INTERESTING ABILITY TO LICK ONESELF

This section is dedicated to those of us who are such gluttons for punishment that we don't think a performance appraisal from a boss or a discussion of our weight with our mothers is enough trauma in our lives.

We insist on putting our lives on paper and sending them out there to be critiqued by people we don't even know.

Have you ever thought "I should write a book?" If so, after stabbing yourself on the hand repeatedly with a seven-pronged fork, you might want to read this section and reconsider. And if you still decide you want to write, welcome to the world's most dysfunctional club...

Does this section apply to you? Answer the following questions:

- Do you enjoy rejection?
- Do you think that being rich is not important?

⁂ Do you think that being sane is not important?

If you want to laugh at me, this section is for you...

From the moment I picked your book up
until I laid it down, I was convulsed
with laughter. Someday I intend reading it.
            -Groucho Marx

Chapter 52

OVERNIGHT SUCCESS...
THE FIFTY-YEAR METHOD

I remember when my first book was released nationally.

It was the moment I had waited for since I wrote my first book at the age of four.

That book, *The Lion Who Tamed the Man*, was a masterpiece of drawings, scribbles, and Hershey Bar smears. That one received rave reviews from my family, who were actually just thrilled that, for once, the Hershey Bar smears were not on the walls.

It was the moment I waited for since the first time I saw a teacher giggle at my writing. I thought it was in answer to my outstanding sense of humor. Little did I know it was actually a giggle at the fact that I thought that if "someone" and "anyone" were correct words, then "noone" should also be a word.

It is the moment my creditors have been waiting for since I discovered the words, "Charge it."

And yet, it seems so funny to me. A person picking a book off the shelf sees only the finished product. They see a series of pages with words and it looks like it appeared overnight. They don't see things like the collection of rejection slips that read like a Friar's Roast. These include lines like:

- Ms. Atwood. I just don't get it. I wish you the best of luck in placing your manuscript elsewhere.
- Dear Author, We cannot see a market for this type of material…
- To: Christee Gabour Atwood. A restraining order is the next step…

And, while those statements were quite encouraging compared to the really nasty rejection letters that I got, I still pushed on. First, I self-published the book. Then I built my sales numbers. I showed that I could get out and promote it. And then I sent it off to more national publishers. The new rejection slips were much more encouraging:

- Ms. Atwood. I still don't get it. Leave me alone.
- Dear Author, You obviously have a lot of relatives who bought your book. We can't count on that sort of insanity nationwide…
- To: Christee Gabour Atwood. You are hereby ordered to appear in court…

So, I went a step further. I spoke to any group who would sit still long enough. I wrote a stage play based on the book. I visited newspapers, radio stations, and television studios. I wrote to Oprah. And finally it came. It was a call from a publisher who was interested. Then, even more shockingly, a contract came. And the most exciting moment of all – the check cleared.

Yes, I'm an overnight success. And it only took 50 years to get there.

※★✷✶✷◆✷※
If you put 100 monkeys into a room with 100 typewriters, the result would be this book. (No offense intended to the monkeys.)

Chapter 53

WRITING A BOOK IN ONE MONTH AND A FEW FIFTHS

Being a glutton for punishment, I decided to participate in National Novel Writing Month (NaNoWriMo) in November.

Basically what happens during this month is this: Otherwise sane people actually sit down and try to write a book in thirty days.

No problem. It's just as simple as getting high schoolers to think you're cool.

In order to celebrate this concept, I'd like to take you through the process one goes through to write a book.

Day One: You sit down and smile. You know that you have accomplished the biggest part. Yes, applying rear to chair is often the hardest part of writing a book.

Day Two: You are not smiling quite as much because you have realized that, although you sat down yesterday, you forgot to put any words on paper.

Day Three: You have a good day. You write some. Then you celebrate by calling everyone you can think of to tell them you are "writing a book".

The rest of Week One: You have a few good days of writing, fueled by the embarrassment you would feel if any of those people called back to ask how the book's going.

And then you begin to create great reasons not to apply rear to chair. The house is dirty. The moon is full. The cat threw up. And a man in a ski mask is knocking at the door, asking for your valuables.

By Week Two, even ski mask guy is laughing as he sees how little you've written. You think that perhaps writing a book is overrated.

You begin to suspect you have West Nile Virus. This keeps you from feeling guilty about the fact that you haven't written in days. But you realize your disease was actually a stomach ache from eating the whole box of "celebratory bon bons," so you lock up and do a whole bunch of pages. That wasn't so hard, so you find it easier to spend your days writing.

Midway through the month you will find that you hate your book. Your main character is bugging you so much that you schedule him for a tax audit. And, after your mother asks if you've gained weight, you have the main character's mother develop laryngitis.

But somewhere in between all this insanity, you find that you actually enjoy creating this world. You discover that your characters will say things that surprise you. You realize you like playing Supreme Being. You decide if it is sunny or snowing. You determine if your world worships love handles. You decide who lives, who dies, and which coworker gets the full body cast and poison ivy. You discover that it doesn't matter if anyone ever reads it. It's your own little world and once created, no one can take it away from you, elect someone you don't like, or invite supermodels to visit.

And those are the best reasons I can imagine to write.

The greatest fiction writing I've ever done? My resume.

Chapter 54

HOW TO WRITE A COLUMN...

It's been twenty years since I started playing as a columnist.

It's been a great ride and I'd like to recommend it to anyone who has lots of time to write and not a great need for money.

To help aspiring columnists prepare for this career choice, I'd like to walk you through the process of writing a column.

First you sit at your beloved keyboard. It is, of course, best if this keyboard is actually attached to something – a computer, a typewriter, a calculator – although that last one tends to make the column a little confusing.

You stare at the blank screen. At this point, your pets will wander into the room to see what the stiff-looking person is doing. Within minutes, you have an animal shedding on your lap, insisting on being fed, or trying to mark you as his territory.

Once you have fed them and employed a lint brush, you are back at that nice keyboard. Now you've actually realized that you need a subject. You begin to think.

Thinking is tiring business, so you head to the kitchen for a cup of coffee. On the way back to your keyboard you realize that the mail has arrived. The next twenty minutes is spent looking through the sales flyers and your bills. Your bills encourage you to ignore the sales flyers. You leave all of these to review later.

Look at that. Your coffee must have evaporated, because every bit of it is gone. You head back to the kitchen.

At this point you realize that your kitchen is a mess, so you take the time to hide the dirty dishes in the dishwasher. Now it looks so nice it invites you to make a small snack for yourself. After this three course meal you're back on your way to write.

Uh oh. A dust bunny is on the loose. You consider vacuuming. Laughing very hard, you continue back to that waiting keyboard.

Your pets are back. One is doing figure eights around your chair. The other is doing his Snoopy imitation, pretending to be a vulture on the back of your chair. After that drop-kicking exercise that always encourages them to find other entertainment, you are back at that darn keyboard.

Outside, you hear kids drag racing down your street. You walk out and stand in your yard, glaring at them as they pass. This does no good whatsoever, but you feel vindicated and turn to go back into the house.

Aha! There is a patch of weeds threatening to choke your rose bush. You feverishly tear the weeds up, talk to the plant, which seems to wilt a little from the garlic in your earlier snack, and finally return to the house.

As you wash your hands, you notice in the mirror that you look terrible. The next half hour is spent trying to "fix your face", a term which means adding spackle to hide the signs of wisdom.

And now you are back at that damn keyboard.

You're no closer to coming up with a subject than before. You think for three minutes, then realize it's starting to get dark. Time for supper.

After supper, you're back at that $%^&*# keyboard, ready to write your column. Seeing that it's now primetime on television, you realize it's much too late to start writing a column today. Tomorrow you'll have to get an earlier start.

And that's all there is to it.

I think I did pretty well,
considering I started out
with nothing but a bunch of blank paper.
                              -Steve Martin

Chapter 55

NATIONAL NOVEL WRITING MONTH, A CHICKEN SUIT, AND MYRON

I now realize that there is much more to be said about the month of November and NaNoWriMo.

In case you missed the chapter, that's short for *National Novel Writing Month*.

Every November, for some reason, I feel the need to participate. That doesn't mean that what comes out of my efforts is a good thing.

Last year I wrote a novel called, *Danger, Deceit, and a Demon ... named Myron*. It's a book that answers the question, "What would happen if you showed up for a job interview and discovered the position was personal assistant to an immortal who is a cross between Shemp and Kevin Sorbo and whose special job is to save the world from evil?"

Needless to say, this book once again reminded me why I don't write a lot of fiction. I'm not really good at sticking with a single plot; a fact which seems to mirror my many career inclinations.

Realizing that I needed 50,000 words, I found myself doing things like having the characters break out into songs such as, "Ninety-nine bottles of beer on the wall." And then they would get confused and start over around twenty-two bottles.

Then, needing even more words, I noticed that one of my main characters developed a stutter. Soon a character appeared who talked like a walking thesaurus. And don't even ask about the character with short-term memory loss...

No, I'm not the best at writing fiction. Besides, my life is sufficiently strange that just telling true stories about it seems comedic enough ... such as the fact that I insisted on writing the aforementioned novel in the window of a bookstore while wearing a chicken suit. Sad, but true. And while I feel I have done many worthwhile things in my lifetime, the episode in the chicken suit is the first time I've gotten national publicity for anything. (You can see the article by going to CBSnews.com and searching for "A Novel Idea".)

So now, as November approaches yet again, I have a dilemma on my hands. How do you top a full body chicken suit? I guess it will be the same step-by-step method I used last year. I'll do intensive research. I'll think about the pros and cons. I'll determine the character that would tie in most effectively with my plot. And then I'll accidentally find the costume while rummaging through a bargain bin in a discount store after drinking two glasses of merlot.

Oh yes, I'll also need that plot thingy. But I'll think about that on November 1st.

Yes, I've spent my life trying to make a positive difference in the world and I'm finally noticed by wearing a chicken suit. Something is not quite right here...

☆★✶✷✶●✷☆

I finished one book while still on pain medication after surgery. It was magnificent writing, however it did require significant editing due to the excessive use of the word "gnaarglespact."

Chapter 56

VIRTUALLY ON TOUR

recently participated in something called a *virtual tour*.

This is where you travel from blog to blog online and answer interview questions.

Some of the questions people asked were interesting, so I thought today I'd share a few of those discussions.

Question: When did you consider yourself a writer? You know what I mean—the time when you realized that you crossed the line from "I want to be a writer" to "I am a writer."

Answer: Oh my gosh! Am I a writer? Well, I actually considered myself a writer from the time I was four years-old and scribbled the masterpiece novel, *The Lion Who Tamed the Man*. But I'm still waiting to feel like an "author." I don't think I've learned the secret handshake yet. I know there has to be one because I've got five books and I'm still not having tea with J.K. Rowling and, as far as John Grisham goes – he never writes, never calls.

Question: Was it always your goal to do a book on midlife crisis?

Answer: Well, actually, it was my goal to write a book that lots and lots of people would want to buy so that I would end up rich enough to hire a maid so I could see what color my carpet really is.

Question: You are an "Ambassador of Mirth." Do you find optimism a tough sell sometimes?

Answer: Great question! And, "Oh Yes!" is the answer. Isn't it a shame that being happy is considered childish?

- Act your age.
- Stop acting like a child.
- Oh, grow up.

So, the message seems to be that if you enjoy life, you're not an adult.

Every day people lock their "joy" into the pocket of their briefcases next to their laptop computers and leave the spring in their step in that pair of tennis shoes that they push out of the way to get to those basic black business shoes. They save their laughter for the occasional email joke or for lunchtime discussions.

What's great is that all it takes is one person with the nerve to laugh at herself or himself to remind us that it's okay to lighten up. I don't mind being that person because I believe that it doesn't lower one's professionalism or credibility to enjoy what you're doing. After all, it's easier to be creative, to be open to unusual ideas for problem-solving, and to be less self-conscious about any mistakes you make when you're laughing.

If that means I'm not acting my age, so be it. Just hand me my rubber chicken and my whoopee cushion and look the other way...

✦ ★ ✶ ✺ ✹ ✦ ✶ ✦

The covers of this book are too far apart.

-Ambrose Bierce

COUCHING THE IDEA OF THERAPY

This section addresses an interesting phenomenon -- trying to act normal, when no one really knows what normal is.

It feels like an episode of the *Twilight Zone* when you realize that it's society that defines normal.

The same society that decided that tall spiked heels on women were a good idea. The society that uses money as a definition of success. The society that brought us the movie *Waterworld* and an invention that allows cats to do "their business" on our toilets.

Does this section apply to you? Answer the following questions:

- Do you experience symptoms of drug interactions when you hear them recited on commercials?
- Do you consider it being assertive when you say, "yes" without adding "sir"?
- Is your result listed as "inconclusive" when you take personality assessments?

If you thought these were silly questions, this section is for you...

Chapter 57

Pressure...
It's Not Just For Cookers Anymore

We seem to think of pressure as a motivator these days.

It's not good enough to say, "I want to do this to the best of my ability for my own personal satisfaction."

I realized this as I explained a project to my husband.

"If I don't do well on this project, it will reflect badly on the company."

"So, do well." He always has an answer.

"But you don't understand the importance of this. If it reflects badly on the company, the company might suffer in fulfilling its mission statement."

"Okay."

"I can tell you still don't get it. If the company suffers in its mission, it could lose business." Sure, I'm spitting a little in my desire to show him my dedication to this purpose, but he's standing far enough away to avoid the biggest drops.

"Wow. Add four horsemen and the world is coming to an end."

"Don't make light of this. If it loses business, the company could have to go through cutbacks."

David has now developed that glaze over his eyes that occurs when I have passed the point of no return. He doesn't answer. But that has never stopped me.

"And if it goes through cutbacks, people may lose their jobs."

He nods. I pretend not to notice that he has picked up a three year-old magazine.

"And if people lose their jobs, they won't buy Christmas presents."

That might have been a snore, but I choose to ignore it.

"And if they don't buy Christmas presents, it will affect the economy."

His head has dropped to his chest. I prefer to think that the rhythmic breathing is a sign of how deeply he is meditating this fact.

"If the economy is affected, there could be a depression."

He jumps at this, or perhaps because of the fact that I am now pacing the room and have stepped on his broken toe. With traces of tears in his eyes, he utters, "I thought it was just a memo that you were working on."

"Right," I screech, and somewhere a dog howls in return. "My inability to write this memo effectively has just caused the next great depression of the twenty-first century!"

"It's a memo asking a person to pick up coffee. I will only affect your caffeine content. Honestly, I think it could use to be affected."

I thought about it. He had a point. I scrapped the memo and opted to call the person, who happily agreed to help.

Sometimes a butterfly flapping its wings only disturbs the butterfly next to him.

※★✷✸✷●✸※
I'm desperately trying to figure out why kamikaze pilots wore helmets.
-Dave Edison

Chapter 58

BEING ASSERTIVE – IF THAT'S OKAY WITH YOU

People laugh so hard when I tell them I'm not assertive.

But then I have to explain to them not to mistake loudness for assertiveness. Just like we shouldn't mistake competence with a big office.

I think the hardest part about being assertive is that sometimes people don't like you when you stand your ground. And being liked is very important to many of us. Then there's Ted Turner, but that's a different matter altogether.

And yes, I understand the difference between assertive and aggressive. But when you've been raised in the South as a "lady", both those words make you feel like you've just punched someone in the stomach.

Guys seem to have it much better when it comes to assertiveness. They are encouraged to be assertive in the business world. They are patted on the back when they are called aggressive in the sports world. However, they are called names that I won't repeat here when their wives catch them trying to use that same assertive behavior at home when it comes to use of the remote control.

But I have digressed again. Let's get back to the "gressing" here...

When I think about my lack of aggressiveness, I always remember one of the first times I went in to ask for a raise.

"I wanted to talk to you about a raise."

"Ow. That hurt."

"Why would that hurt?"

"It's an insult. It means you feel that I'm not treating you right."

"No. It's just that times change. It's time for a raise."

"But if I give you one, I'll have to give everyone on the staff one."

"I'm good at keeping secrets."

"Oh, but if they see you able to buy fancy things like bread and meat that's not marked for quick sale, they'll know."

"Well, maybe it's time for everyone to get a raise."

"Now you're just talking crazy."

"But sir, I need a raise. I'm pretty sure minimum wage has been raised since I started here."

"Do you want us to have to close down? That's what will happen if I give raises willy nilly around here."

"Well I certainly wouldn't want that. But maybe you could give willy raises and leave out the nilly."

"You're a socialist, aren't you?"

"No sir."

And finally he said those words that are the crushing blow to any southern lady. "You're awfully aggressive today."

We ended the meeting with no raise and I agreed to simonize his car. I just couldn't handle being called aggressive.

Today, I am much more assertive. Things would have been different in that negotiation. I would have refused to leave without some change – probably dimes and nickels. I would have argued a little harder for my right to afford all four food groups. I would have suggested nilly raises instead of willy. And when he called me aggressive, I would have been so proud that I would have called my mother…

My last good reference letter said,
"Plays well with others. Doesn't eat paste."

Chapter 59

An Impostor With Restless Leg Syndrome

Symptoms make me sick.

Really.

I realized this as I watched television the other day and every time a commercial came on, I felt I had the symptoms they described.

A cold medicine ad had me sniffling and coughing. A little later some guy told me my dry eyes were a "condition." And later that evening, I punted the cat off the couch and shrugged, "Restless leg syndrome."

I am very susceptible to outside influences. I think the pioneers had it easy because there were no advertising people to tell them that it wasn't okay to have dry skin, body odor, and bleeding from the ears. And psychological symptoms are the worst.

Psychology classes in college were really bad for me. I studied agoraphobia and suddenly decided I wasn't lazy, I was just afraid to leave the house. I found out that I had an inferiority complex ... and that mine was a bigger inferiority complex than anyone else's. I realized that there was something wrong with me because I didn't hate my parents. And when I signed up for "Abnormal Psychology", my family talked me into dropping the class after only one session. Good call there.

But not too long ago, I was reading a psychology book and discovered something that really rang true. It's called the *Impostor Phenomenon*. It's where you think that everything you've accomplished is an accident. That your success is just a fluke, and that, at any minute, your house of cards may fall and everyone will see that you're not really any good at anything. Or they'll see you in your junior high school underwear – oh wait, I think that's a different fear.

And so, once again, I'm working on my positive affirmations.

"Christee, good job on that seminar." My friend patted me on the back. I choked back the urge to say, "You have incredibly low standards." Instead I nodded and smiled.

A construction worker whistled and I did not immediately look behind me to see whom he was admiring. I just nodded and smiled. (Okay, honestly, behind me was a college student with hair that was too big and a shirt that was too small. But I ignored that fact.)

And when my mother told me, "Well, your last column was a little better," I took it for what it was worth, nodded and smiled.

I acknowledged the fact that I can actually know things without having a framed certificate to say that I know them. Just because my degree doesn't say "BS in Customer Service," doesn't mean that I don't know the right way to treat a guest in my home. Because it doesn't say "Master of

Fine Talking," doesn't mean I can't speak without spitting on someone. And, even though I don't have a degree in Office Management, I can actually survive an entire day in an office environment without a single call to 911.

And so, I am working to overcome my Impostor Phenomenon. Next week I'll start working on that restless leg thing.

A reporter asked Brigadier General Wilma Vaught: "What did you want to be when you grew up?" She answered, "In charge."

Chapter 60

This Tape... And My Reputation... Will Self-Destruct

The scariest thing happened to me the other day.

I turned on my little digital recorder and discovered it had accidentally recorded me at home earlier that morning.

It started out with me talking to myself ... and answering.

My great examples of self-talk included, "I've seen better-looking hair on a baboon's bottom." "If my upper arms flap any more I'm going to take off." "Oh well, I guess I'll have to do."

Then I started singing. From nowhere came the '70s tune, "There's a Dead Skunk in the Middle of the Road and It's Stinkin' to High Heaven" by Loudon Wainwright III. Trust me, it was as bad a song as the title indicates. And my rendition of it had neighborhood dogs howling.

As if that weren't bad enough, I then apparently felt the need to start a conversation with my poor husband. I felt so bad as I listened to the recording of my inane chatter.

"David, do you still like me?"

"Love you," he insists.

"Why?"

I think I detect a small groan before he answers. "Because you're you."

"That's sweet, but I want real."

"You're a good soul. You make me laugh. You're my best friend."

"Yeah, but…" I begin.

More groans from David.

"I'm high maintenance, aren't I?" I ask.

If I didn't know better, I'd think the next sound I heard on the recording was his shriek. But it must have just been his chair creaking. "No, you're not high maintenance to me. Just to yourself."

I'm silent for a minute. Apparently I was letting this soak in. "What would you like me to change about me?"

He is really quick on this one, "The way you treat yourself."

"Good answer," I acknowledge. "Now, how about something else?"

I can tell from his distracted voice that he is trying to do something else, or maybe he's slipping into the coma that happens when I decide to psychoanalyze one or both of us.

"Nothing." To reinforce this, he's now humming Billy Joel's "Just The Way You Are" as he tries to type on his computer. I ignore this subtle dismissal hint and continue.

"There's got to be something I can work on," I insist.

"Okay, you could learn to relax a little more," he finally concedes.

"Oh, I know that. After all, I've gone to a mini-Zen retreat. And I used my speed-reading to get through a book on relaxation techniques. And I got the instant guide to meditation..." I stopped in mid-sentence. "I'm a know-it-all, aren't I?" I ask him.

"If you were, you wouldn't have to ask."

Wow. He's getting really good at this. I finally give up. "Thanks David. I feel much better. I'll work on relaxing."

I am singing a Christmas song while moving to the next room, where apparently, I come upon my sleeping cats.

"Hey kids." I must have plopped onto the couch next to them, judging from the strained squeaks from both the couch and my knees. "Is there anything you'd like me to change about myself?"

The hissing and sounds of running paws are the last things on the recorder.

I learned a valuable lesson from listening to my ramblings, self-incriminations, off-tune humming, and non-stop talking on this recorder. I just can't decide what lesson it was. Either: a) I need to stop feeling the need to talk constantly, b) I need to invest in more hours of therapy, or c) I just need to stop carrying a recorder.

I give until it hurts. Unfortunately I have a very low pain threshold.

Chapter 61

The Expense of Being Brilliant

A ccents are expensive.

Allow me to elucidate. Or I'll explain if you'd like.

When a telemarketer calls, I know how to get rid of them. I simply offer to let them talk to my mommy and they never call back.

If a telemarketer gets past that landmine and is brave enough to start extolling the features of their new phone, television, or banking service, I yell "Fire" and slam the phone down.

If they are persistent enough to call back, I answer the phone, "Atwood residence, Chief Nurse speaking". I explain that Mrs. Atwood has been stricken with a severe case of Leevmeeuhloanitis and cannot be disturbed. Many notice that the Chief Nurse sounds suspiciously like the ill party, but few are crass enough to voice that realization.

Those who do mention that fact receive a severe reprimand, "Well, of course I sound like her. She's my twin." At this point they start trying to sell their service to the twin who quickly explains that she does not speak English and hangs up.

All of this to avoid saying "no." I've never claimed to be an assertive person.

"So," you might be asking, "how in the world does this lead to a realization about accents?"

It all happened when I had to call a software company to register my newly purchased software at 9:20 this morning.

"Good morning," a delightfully British-accented voice spoke. "My name is Omar. How may I service you?"

Omar sounded cute which meant that the first answer that came to my mind was not entirely appropriate.

"I need to register my software."

"Brilliant," answered Omar. He said it with such gusto that I immediately felt smarter. "Are you in the states?"

I loved that states thing. It felt so worldly. "Yes."

"Brilliant" again. My IQ had now moved up by 3.5 points and I determined that he was correct. I must be brilliant. We registered my software and then he began the obligatory upsell.

Understand, I've been attacked by the best. The people at AbWheel tried to sell me a second one for a reduced price. Why I would want to roll in two directions at once was beyond me. (Note to self: Never use an AbWheel after application of multiple margaritas. I did a face plant much like Mikie of LSU in the 2009 College World Series. Great catch, Mikie...)

Oops, I got off track again. ADHD.

The point is that I know how to stop a person from upselling me and I do it frequently. But this time, with

Omar, his British accent and expressions … well, I found myself not only listening, but asking questions.

Those were some expensive questions. Yeah, I bought.

As I explained to Omar, it was so pleasant not to be bullied into buying like they do on this side of "the pond" (yeah, I was feeling the bond by now) and I looked forward to calling him again to upgrade my software further. Omar was most appreciative. I think there might have even been another "brilliant" somewhere in there.

If this had been a person with a Jersey inflection or a Texas twang, I don't think those "brilliants" would have made me buy. It was the accent that sold me.

Note to self: After my tea and scones this afternoon I'll have to remind myself to deal only with businesses in the states. It's too expensive to work with accents.

Anyone who lives within their means suffers from a lack of imagination.
-Oscar Wilde

Chapter 62

SIDE EFFECTS OF CHRISTEE

I think we should all have warning labels. It would make life so much easier.

I've realized this as I've struggled with the fact that I have the attention span of a Chihuahua on crack. Yeah, it's probably that ADHD stuff. However, it's also a great excuse for so many things like the fact that no one in my family has gotten a birthday card from me since those that I scribbled in crayon with misspelled words and silly pictures. (I think that was in the '80's.)

If a label can remind me not to take a pill on an empty stomach, why can't a label tell people not to expect me to finish a sentence before I move on to the next? I get bored. After all, that other sentence is old and I have newer thoughts that often contradict the old ones.

And so, I have created an instruction/warning label to attach to myself.

Directions:

Take no more than once a day and in very small doses. Large doses of Christee may cause various side effects including, but not limited to, ringing in the ears, nausea, headache, confusion, dizziness, consideration of a monastic lifestyle, restless leg syndrome, changing of political parties, and an intense desire to chew off one's restless leg to escape.

Use earplugs as needed when dealing with Christee. This is necessary due to the fact that Christee has not yet learned to use her "indoor voice" and has been known to cackle at a tone that cracks glass and ruptures appendixes and sometimes even the table of contents.

Warnings:

Remember that if you don't see Christee write something down, she will not do it. It is recommended that, for important tasks, you use a permanent marker and write them directly on her hand. This method was used successfully to ensure she remembered to breathe and blink.

To ensure proper distribution, remove snack foods from within arm's reach of Christee. It is not that Christee is a voracious eater. It is simply that she forgets she already ate some and will continue to reopen the bag and eat five pieces of whatever it is until it is all gone. This is especially unfortunate with bags of dried prunes.

Do not say, "Take a look at this funny article" to Christee when she is working. If you do, not only does the information in her head leak out of her left ear, but she will also take what you are looking at, analyze it to the point that it is no longer funny, and try to figure out how to make money off of it.

Do not talk to Christee in the late evening or before bedtime. This may result in poor sleep patterns, dreams in which your boss gives your performance review in front of your family and friends in the Superdome, and diarrhea.

Do not expect Christee to be silent for more than 3.37 seconds at a time. This is biologically impossible, even if she has laryngitis. In this case, she will act out everything in charades using the cat, four tablespoons, and a head of cabbage.

Do not operate heavy machinery, cars, or telephones under the influence of Christee, as this may lead to a desire to beat your head repeatedly on these objects. Alcohol may intensify this effect.

If an overdose of Christee is suspected, immediately call her mother to commiserate.

I wish they would stop all animal testing. They have trouble filling in those little circles and it stresses them out.

My tombstone will read,
"Finally... a place with quiet neighbors."

FAILURE...
MAKES GREAT STORIES FOR LATE NIGHT TV

This section focuses on failure.

It's easy to find. It's the thing that happens one more time right before success.

And the cool thing is that the more times it happens, the better the success story sounds.

Do we like stories of a person who sold that bestseller the first time it was sent to a publisher?

No. We like the story of *Zen and the Art of Motorcycle Maintenance* that was turned down 121 times. It tells us there's still hope for us on attempt number 120.

Failure. It's at the beginning of every great American success story.

Does this section apply to you? Answer the following questions:

- Do you believe failure is never final?
- However, do you accept that failure on a final exam is final?
- Do you feel confused by the first two questions?

If you have ever thought, "If at first you don't succeed, don't tell anybody," this section is for you…

✯★✵✸✵⬥✵✯
I have not failed. I've just found 10,000 ways that won't work.
-Thomas A. Edison

Chapter 63

FAILING YOUR WAY TO SUCCESS

Yes, I get really disgusted with myself and think I've made so many mistakes that I am to success what Paris Hilton is to gracious living.

It's at those times that I have to stop and remind myself that failures have created some of the greatest victories in our history.

If some new type of glue hadn't failed, we'd never have gotten sticky notes and our computer monitors would look terribly lonesome.

Ice cream cones wouldn't have been discovered if someone hadn't ordered too few cups at a World's Fair and decided to use thin waffles instead.

Potato chips wouldn't have been created if a cook hadn't gotten disgusted with a customer. The person kept sending back a plate of potatoes to have them cooked further. Finally the cook sliced a bunch of potatoes paper thin and cooked them to a crisp. He threw salt on them and sent them back to the customer, sure the customer would hate them. The customer liked them so much he ordered more. Tah dah! A snack was born.

Chocolate chip cookies were a mistake too. The cook ran out of bakers chocolate and broke some pieces of sweetened chocolate into the dough. She thought that, when baked, the pieces would melt into the dough and make chocolate cookies. Little did she know that years later women everywhere would forget about cooking the dough and eat it straight as a remedy for boyfriend troubles.

So, without these mistakes, we'd have missed out on a lot of joy. Thinner, yes, but that's a different discussion.

And if Christopher Columbus hadn't failed, we'd all be living in the East Indies. We'd have great spices, but where would they fit a Disneyworld there?

If the mother of Michael Nesmith of *The Monkees* hadn't been such a bad typist and decided to use white paint to cover her mistakes, she would never have thought of inventing liquid paper to cover her errors. And those of us who grew up typing school research papers on typewriters would have been retyping those #$%^&! pages over and over again.

And then there was the movie, *Waterworld*. Maybe sometimes the lesson is just to make us glad that it wasn't our failure?

Every failure leads us to some new discovery – even if it's just the discovery of a way not to do that in the future. So why are we so scared to admit they happened?

Perhaps the invention of erasers was not such a good thing after all. They let us pretend our failures, our mistakes, and our false starts, never existed. If we had to scratch through them and still see them in the background, we'd remember them, learn from them, and be humbled by them.

I think Thomas Edison summed this whole thing up best when he said, "Genius? Nothing! Sticking to it is the genius. I've failed my way to success."

So there's our moral for the day. Don't erase mistakes. Put a line through them. Celebrate those mistakes and the lessons learned from them.

And then sign them with someone else's name...

Know yourself. Don't accept your dog's admiration as conclusive evidence that you are wonderful.
              -Ann Landers

Chapter 64

LESSONS FROM A CHAGRINED CAPUCHIN

I received an email today from Enis the Chagrined Capuchin.

Yes, it was actually from my husband, but he assumes other personalities when he realizes I'm in a bad mood and it will take the "big guns" to cheer me up.

So, Enis, being the cute little capuchin monkey that he apparently is, sent me an email card to make me feel better. It worked. Why can't all of life be that simple?

When I'm in a bad mood, why can't I just say, "I'm in a bad mood. Get over it, Self." Then I could walk happily on my way and forget it.

And when I'm wrong, why can't I just say it? If we all got everything right, the world would be pretty boring and there'd be no topics for talk shows. So why is it so hard to admit these things?

"I was wrong. Your idea is better." Wow, that didn't hurt at all. Why don't I say it more often?

"I was stupid." Yup, this is one I should have said after I tried practicing psychology without a license on a friend once.

Or, "I really thought a diet book was a good birthday gift. I was mistaken." Self-explanatory.

I'm not alone. Companies spend millions of dollars trying to hide their mistakes instead of apologizing and taking their lumps. They waste time using shredders and they fire the people who tell them they're making errors. Instead they could simply say, "Wow, we really messed that one up!" Then they could have a good laugh, pay some fines, spend a few years in jail learning a new trade, and move on. But instead, they waste all that time trying to rent politicians and other officials to get them out of trouble without anyone knowing it.

I've messed up so many times that making mistakes has become an art form for me. I've hurt people without realizing it because of my "open mouth, insert Nike" talent. I've said more wrong things than Union General John Sedgwick, whose last words were "They couldn't hit an elephant at this dist…"

I've had worse ideas than the person who said Beta recorders would beat out VHS. I've worn outfits that should have been illegal on a person who was working out of the elastic end of her closet. And yet, it takes me ages to realize that I need to say, "Oops … sorry…" and get back to work on my growth. Because that's what all of this is about.

I have lessons to learn. If I didn't, I wouldn't be here. I'd be some ethereal floating creature that watches over the world and snickers knowingly at car dealers who do their own commercials. I'd be a superior being that never needs to be quietly told that a breath mint is in order. I'd be so perfect that no one would ever be tempted to wave at me with a single digit to explain that my driving leaves something to be desired. But instead I'm making mistakes. That means I'm still trying new things. Isn't that a good thing?

And so, the thing that Enis and I remind myself is that victories are fun, but failures are better. I learn something from the failures.

That's what this journey is all about…

Always go to other people's funerals; otherwise they won't come to yours.

-Yogi Berra

Chapter 65

PRINCIPLES AND VICES OF PRINCIPLES

Have you ever done something completely silly because of a principle?

No, I don't mean an important principle like life, liberty, or the pursuit of happiness.

I mean a ridiculous principle like, "The ad for the product said this would work and I'm going to keep doing this until it actually does."

That's exactly what I did this morning when I vacuumed my carpet. (Yes, let's take a moment to move past the shock of Christee actually vacuuming. What can I say? It was a full moon.)

This morning as I vacuumed, I found the smallest little piece of a leaf ... and the vacuum cleaner didn't pick it up. I tried again. Still no luck. I kicked at it with my foot to move it into a better position. Nope. And then I reached down and picked it up, moved it and tried to vacuum over it again. I broke it into smaller pieces and rolled over it once more. Then I finally picked the pieces up and "fed" them to the vacuum cleaner.

Amazing. I could have picked it up and tossed it in the trash five minutes before – the first time I tried to move that smallest little piece of leaf. But it was the principle. It was a vacuum cleaner and it was supposed to make life easier by doing the work for me.

I find that I do many things in the name of "principle" that make no sense.

I once fought with the television remote control for a quarter of an hour, finally resorting to changing the batteries to make the darn thing work. All the while I was getting more and more perturbed because I wanted to watch my show. No, I had not walked to the television to turn it on. Instead I missed the first ten minutes of the show fighting over a principle with an inanimate object.

I do this with people sometimes. I have almost had wrecks because – doggone it – I was in the right. So, even though somebody was honking at me or waving with nine fingers hidden, I was not giving up my pursuit of the rightful use of the roadway. I'm surprised my insurance company hasn't come up with a "high-handed overly-principled" driver rate.

I've spent hours searching for things that cost less than a dollar, refusing to buy a new one because I know that mine is here "somewhere." (Definition of somewhere: The place where things hide until right after the moment when you finally break down and buy another.)

I've spent many, many hours searching for "shortcuts" on my computer when it would have been only one extra keystroke to do the function the "long way." It was the principle. There was a shortcut and I was going to use it ... even if it took longer.

There are many more examples I could cite. However, a modicum of self-respect doesn't allow me to tell them all. Suffice to say, one of them included using hand-held hedge trimmers to edge my yard because I didn't think I should have to buy a separate machine for that. (Note to self: A doctor visit costs more than an edger.)

Principles. Vice Principles. I'm still learning from them without even getting called into their offices.

I will no longer consider that "fur" on my ceiling fan as an artistic statement.

Chapter 66

Journaling, ADHD, and Shiny Objects

For the last few decades, I've made a practice of writing in a journal every morning.

It's a habit I can't recommend strongly enough. I use it to clear my head, to record my dreams, and to avoid doing any housecleaning.

Today I decided to review some of my old journals and see if there are any recurring themes, discover any good quotes, and laugh at my frequent promises to exercise regularly.

- 1983 – Los Angeles is an exciting place to live. Today I was surprised to find I was the only woman in the restaurant, The Yukon Mining Company. And how did that perfectly coifed waiter know I was from out of town?

- 1984 – If I cut out my negative self-talk, I'd have self-laryngitis.

- 1985 – Commodore 64 computers are the best things in the world. Nothing will ever replace these!

- 1986 – If I were on a deserted island and could take only one thing, what would I take? A bartender.

- ✯ 1987 – I love small, yipping, hyperactive dogs. I need the field goal practice.

- ✯ 1988 – I can't seem to focus on any one thing.
- ✯ 1989 – I envy the man who whistles while shoveling manure.
- ✯ 1990 – Hmmm, I seemed to have gained a few pounds.
- ✯ 1991 – Today I have discovered that I don't have an "indoor voice."
- ✯ 1992 – Playing it by ear doesn't work as well when you're tone deaf.
- ✯ 1993 – Hmmm, I seemed to have gained a few pounds.
- ✯ 1994 – Atlanta is a fun place to live. It reminds me of Louisiana without the good food. I'm going back to Louisiana.
- ✯ 1995 – Back in Louisiana. Hmmm, I seemed to have gained a few pounds.
- ✯ 1996 – I have a problem sticking with any one thing.
- ✯ 1997 – I looked great this morning ... Then I put on my glasses.
- ✯ 1998 – Life is too short to read weak books and too long to hold strong grudges.
- ✯ 1999 – Today my ship came in! Should I worry that it's named "Titanic II"?
- ✯ 2000 – I wonder if I have ADHD?
- ✯ 2001 - When my shoulders keep bumping my ears, I know I'm stressed.
- ✯ 2002 - All the world's a stage ... and today I have stage fright.

- 2003 – Why do I have to turn down the car radio to see better?
- 2004 – Hmmm, I seemed to have gained a zip code.
- 2005 – I have the attention span of a gnat.
- 2006 – I have the attention span of a gnat with ADHD.
- 2007 – Problems are just opportunities wearing trench coats and schnocker glasses.
- Today – I have the attent... Hey, look, a shiny object...

Nope, no recurring themes there.

And so, from my journals I discover that I, like the noble onion, have many layers. Some of them are actually deep. Some of them produce a giggle. Some of them have that papery skin attached. (I have no idea what that means.) And cutting into some of them can make tears flow.

Guess I'll close them and open a new book today.

This is not a novel to be tossed aside lightly.
It should be thrown with great force.
                                    -Dorothy Parker

Chapter 67

I Prefer to Give My Age in Dog Years

I think my age looks better in dog years. I am a little over seven now.

By this age I thought I was supposed to be mature. I thought I would know what I wanted to be when I grew up. I thought I would have a savings account. Hmmm... Zero out of three isn't good, is it?

But it's another exciting stage of my life. A stage where my body makes more noises than that mysterious rattle under my dashboard. Where I've decided that if God intended me to stay one size for the rest of my life, he wouldn't have invented "one size fits all." Where I've realized that the "challenges" in life are more exciting than if everything went right.

What kind of "challenges"? I'm so glad you asked...

- I am occupationally challenged. My resume is now too long to be listed job by job. Now it is just "Highlights" pages. And no one seems entertained by the listing of my former bosses as Harpo, Groucho, and Dopey.
- I am mechanically challenged. I spent three hours trying to figure out how to operate a Mickey Mouse CD player. And two hours of that were spent just trying to get the wrapper off the CD that I wanted to play.
- I'm visually challenged. I now own seven pairs of reading glasses but I can never see well enough to find where I left them.
- I am intellectually challenged. My idea of literature now includes Harry Potter, paperbacks with bare-chested men on them, the funny pages, and Cliff Notes of things I should have read in high school.
- I am domestically challenged. I have finally accepted the fact that my house will never be really clean unless it's a rental and I want the deposit back before moving.
- I am memory challenged. I remember myself in high school as quiet, shy, and reasonably cute. One glance at my yearbook reminds me of that ecology sit-in I staged with my bullhorn, my AA-sized chest, and my DD-sized nose.
- I'm recreationally challenged. I have not taken up a single hobby in the last ten years that has not given me some sort of injury. Examples? Baseball: injured elbow. Walking: twisted knee. Gardening: poison ivy. Writing: carpal tunnel syndrome. Couch: oversized rear end.

In Celebration of Elastic Waistbands

- I am focus challenged. I will start cooking a meal, decide to clean out the utensils drawer, run to look something up on the internet, then hurry to the living room to see what it is I'm hearing on television. It usually takes the smoke alarm for me to remember the first item I was working on.
- I'm hormonally challenged. My moods have more swings than a mid-city playground. And if I don't get my prescriptions refilled on time, my pharmacist shows up at my door with them and a box of chocolates.

And finally, I'm goal challenged. Every time I think I see the light at the end of the tunnel, I realize that Grandma is standing next to it...

You know you're getting old when you stoop to tie your shoelaces and wonder what else you could do while you're down there.
                                                            -George Burns

✲★✶✳✶●✳✲

Columbus didn't get to the place he was supposed to be going. When he got back he didn't know where he'd been. He did it on someone else's money. And he got a day named after him. Sort of lowers the bar, doesn't it?

BALANCED & UNBALANCED LESSONS

This section sums up some of the many lessons we learn as we go through life.

Every year we can update this section, because if we're doing things right, we're still making mistakes every single day.

And if we're doing things really right, we're learning from those mistakes. If we're not learning from those mistakes, we're probably the television network executive who cancelled *Frank's Place*.

Does this section apply to you? Answer the following questions:

- Did you learn the valuable lesson that the words *hot wax*, *underarm*, and *at home* should never be used in the same sentence?
- Do you believe that you learn more from mistakes than victories?
- Do you still prefer not to learn so much?

If you are glancing to see how close you are to the end of this book, this section is for you...

Chapter 68

Thinking, Rethinking, and Drinking

I've noticed that there are sayings we use every day that don't make a lot of sense ... and some that could really use some rethinking.

So today I decided to take some old sayings and try to make them new ... sort of like I do with turkey after the holidays.

- Experience is the best teacher. But I'd prefer a substitute teacher if it lessens the number of bruises I get.
- Easier said than done. Unless you're the boss in the office.
- The bigger, the better. If this is true, then why are there so many diet programs?
- You can't take it with you. But you can sure use it up to make sure that no one else gets it.

- You can't teach an old dog new tricks. Unless you have the right kind of doggy treats.
- The journey of a thousand miles begins with someone else saying, "While you're there, would you get me…"
- Wearing my heart on my sleeve. Obviously, the surgery wasn't successful.
- Like taking candy from a baby. Does this mean it includes wiping drool and listening to a lot of crying?
- You can say that again. But strangely enough, when you do, they get bored.
- Brevity is the soul of wit. And yet, people still insist on sending those really long email jokes.
- Early to bed and early to rise. Means you never see prime time television … which might just be a good thing.
- Eat, drink, and be merry, for tomorrow we die. Gee, there's a cheery person to party with.
- Give him enough rope and he'll hang himself. Or he'll do macramé.
- Ignorance is bliss. Boy, is my life blissful…
- The meek shall inherit the earth. But only after the brash have worn the heck out of it.
- Practice makes perfect. So, when do we stop calling it practice and start calling it perfecting?
- Practice what you preach. Better yet, just don't preach.

- Slow but steady wins the race. So why does everyone insist on passing everyone else on the interstate?
- Stone walls do not a prison make. However, if those stone walls are connected by electric fences, barbed wire, and padlocks, you're pretty well on the way.
- Time heals all wounds. Time is money. Does this mean that money heals all wounds?
- Where there's smoke, there's a group of employees on break.
- The early bird gets the worm. But who wants worms?
- You can catch more flies with honey than with vinegar. Please refer to the note about early birds and replace "worms" with "flies."
- You can't go home again. Tell that to a college kid with a bag of laundry.

My apologies to the intelligent individuals who made these statements. In my defense, the recycling of my Thanksgiving turkeys is usually equally uninspiring...

Outside of a dog, a book is man's best friend. Inside of a dog it's too dark to read.
                                    -Groucho Marx

Chapter 69

THE BALANCING ACT

I looked at my friend's planner and cringed.

"You have every minute scheduled."
"Yes," she said and smiled. "Isn't that efficient?"
"You scheduled 'Fun' at 5:25 p.m."
She nodded. "I'm working to achieve balance in my life."
"But what if you don't want to have 'Fun' at 5:25 p.m.?"
"I have to have discipline. Even if I don't enjoy it, I will have 'Fun' at 5:25 p.m." She smiled and went off for her scheduled 2:22 p.m. restroom break.

We are working so hard to give the impression of balance that most of us are in danger of becoming well-balanced robots.

I do it too. I make lists in every category of my life every week. I have my family goals, my physical goals, my spiritual goals, my business goals, and so on. I know I won't get to them all. When will I accept that there are going to be weeks when I won't have time to work on that goal to become a thinner couch potato?

I think that's where I miss the point. When I have a major project for work, I need to realize that my housecleaning goal of wrangling dust bunnies will suffer. When that project is over, I can return to goals I want to tackle next. It's not about balance. It's about choices.

The next thing I notice in this category is how often I use the words, "I have to..." I say them and suddenly I feel unbalanced. I feel like I'm being forced to do something. "I have to finish this project, so I'll be late getting home today." "I have to go to this meeting or they'll vote for me as chairman of some new committee." "I have to eat this chocolate bar..." Sorry, no reason. That one just slipped in.

I choose to. Those are the words that make me feel balanced. Whenever I change my language from "I have to" to "I choose to," I suddenly feel in control. I practiced it recently.

Instead of "I have to clean the cat litter box", I said, "I choose to clean the cat litter box. It will make it possible for me to enter this room without holding my breath."

Wow. That felt good.

Instead of "I have to go to a meeting" I said, "I am choosing to go to a meeting today to earn money for luxuries like a new jacket, a vacation, and the electricity bill."

Absolutely wonderful.

I didn't say, "I have to meet with this person even though I'd rather be forced to watch Old Navy commercials." Instead I said, "I'm choosing to meet with this person even though I'd rather be forced to watch Old Navy commercials."

I feel so balanced, I'm ready to join the Flying Wallendas.

✯★✶✹✶✿✹✯
You make the beds, you do the dishes, and six months later you have to start all over again.
- Joan Rivers

Chapter 70

WE ARE NOT ALONE

Yes, from the title of this chapter, you might think this refers to aliens.

You should be so lucky. Then it might actually be interesting.

But no, today I realized something very important and wanted to share it with you.

We are not alone.

We all have those times when we think we are the only ones going through our particular woes. The good news is these are actually the times we have the most in common with our fellow man, woman, or transgender individual. I've realized this every time I've heard someone say, "I thought that was just me!"

Unfortunately it also means that, when I think that my particular brand of brilliance is so unique that no one else could share it, I am mistaken.

I was reminded of this last week when I happened upon a book by a fellow named Jerome K. Jerome. I was amazed to find someone who had voiced so many of the same things I have written about in columns. The only difference was that his chapters were written over a century ago.

In 1890, this delightful fellow wrote the following in the preface to his book:

"What readers ask now-a-days in a book is that it should improve, instruct, and elevate. This book wouldn't elevate a cow. I cannot conscientiously recommend it for any useful purposes whatever. All I can suggest is, that when you get tired of reading "the best hundred books," you may take this up for a half an hour. It will be a change."

For the intro to my next book, I may just put "Ditto."

Jerome also had some wonderful comments, such as "I like work: it fascinates me. I can sit and look at it for hours."

On the all-important concept of truth, he stated, "It is always the best policy to speak the truth--unless, of course, you are an exceptionally good liar."

You can't beat philosophy like that.

And so, today, I am prompted to share my own thoughts that have probably been said much more eloquently a million times before:

- My goal for today is to stop thinking I'm God's intern.
- No matter how saintly the person, when he kicks his toe on the couch leg, the first words he thinks are not, "Oh, zoinks!"
- Have you heard the line comedians use to encourage people to come back and see their show again? They say, "I'll be here all week." When I did stand-up

comedy, my line was, "I'll be here all week. Better come back next week."

* I catch illnesses so easily; I'm scared to watch the medical channel.
* I love to have other people tell me their opinions. It gives me a chance to catch my breath.
* I consider the really bad words I write like an opera singer clearing his throat before singing. Those words have to come out before the pretty ones do...
* My goal in life is to find as many opportunities as possible for my inner child and my outer adult to exchange roles.

I know if I look through quotation encyclopedias, I'll probably find lots of people who have said virtually the same things. I am not unique. And as humbling as that thought is, it's also darn comforting.

✦ ★ ✳ ✳ ✳ ◆ ✳ ✦

What I am looking for is a blessing not in disguise.

-Jerome K. Jerome

Chapter 71

Refrigerator Box Redecorating

I am a fairly prolific writer. That doesn't mean "good". It just means I've killed a lot of trees.

I've been a columnist for newspapers and magazines since 1989. I've written seven books, five of them in the last 2.5 years. Number eight is waiting to be adopted. I've written confusing articles, scathing editorials, adventure stories that lurk in my desk drawers, and epic emails that could be considered novels.

People ask me how I write so much so quickly.

Easy.

Other people worry about things like quality plots, nouns and verb agreement, proper word usage and spelling, a sense of perspective, confirmed facts, interesting content, and making mortgage payments. By ignoring all of those concepts and being prepared to move into a refrigerator box at any given moment, I've become a prolific writer.

I guess for me, life is all about trade-offs. I could have friends who actually hear from me and a life where I do things other than type. I could have financial security. I could have a house where the floor color is not "dust". But I made a decision. I want to get my thoughts onto paper more than I want to get clean sheets onto the bed.

And while this sounds silly and more than a little lazy, it just seems right for me.

Today is a great example of that. I have some place to be. It's an appointment at a specific time that is drawing perilously near. And yet I find myself yanking my laptop out of its bag and standing here at the kitchen counter typing this chapter as it comes to me.

Yes, I admit that the kitchen is adorned with a few days of dishes, something gray and furry growing on the counter, and a lump on the floor that I'm not getting close enough to investigate but that I strongly suspect has a correlation to the satisfied-looking cat sitting in the doorway.

That's my life. I'd rather write than be productive and sanitary. I'd rather laugh than be deep and quoted. I'd rather eat than ... well, pretty much anything. That sums me up.

I could say that there's a deep lesson to this chapter, but no. I guess it's more of a lesson from the shallow end of the pool. It's that decisions and trade-offs in life aren't always fun, but at least they cut through the noise and get us back to what truly matters.

In closing, I'd like to ask a question. What would you move into a refrigerator box for? Have you done anything toward it today?

Just a thought.

✯ ★ ✳ ✺ ✶ ◆ ✺ ✯

Either he's dead or my watch has stopped.
-Groucho Marx

Chapter 72

The Cynic's Quiz

I believe we all have a little cynic in us.

Yes, no matter how rosy and optimistic we are, there is a side of us that laughs harder at the legislative reports in the newspaper than the comic pages.

A side that wonders how much the "free item" we have just won will cost us.

A side that believes the most important thing we learned in school was not to run our hands on the underside of a desk.

The quiz that follows will help you determine your level of cynicism.

Simply count the number of items below that you have ever wondered about…

- At what age does the stuff in my house change from being "junk" to being "collectibles?"
- Why is it considered bad to have "a dog's life" when they get food, petting, and housing without ever having to work in a cubicle?
- Does my toilet seat have an alarm that automatically makes my phone ring?
- What would I do if I spent my entire life keeping up with the Joneses and then discovered that the Joneses are axe murderers?
- Why are there Braille instructions at my drive-through ATM?
- If exercise is so healthy for us, why is it called "tennis elbow" instead of "beer drinker's elbow?"
- What's wrong with answering the phone, "What fresh hell is this?"
- Do they really expect me to let brownies cool fifteen minutes?
- On all those home videos shows, why are people videotaping someone painting a house while standing on a rickety ladder?
- Is assault justifiable when someone asks me when I'm due when I'm not pregnant?
- If opposites attract, why do we use "irreconcilable differences" as grounds for divorce?
- Why is a poor person with strange habits labeled "crazy," but a wealthy person with those same habits is called "eccentric?"

Scoring:
- ✣ **1-3** You are slightly cynical. You believe that 33% of the information you get from television is false. You doubt many of things you read on the internet.
- ✣ **4-7** You are a cynic. You believe that 66% of what you see on television is false and that reality television is one of the plagues predicted in the Bible. You know that those internet products can't really increase the size of any body part.
- ✣ **8 +** You are a certified cynic. The last time you were fooled by the media was the "great toilet paper shortage of 1974." You know that those junk emails you get from a "young sexy single" are actually from a middle-aged guy in Iowa with a bad toupee and an Oedipal Complex. And you know that the most frightening thing in the world is not nuclear war, but the thought of Simon Cowell being cloned.

It is always the best policy to speak the truth, unless, of course, you are an exceptionally good liar.
 -Jerome K. Jerome

Chapter 73

NEVER WATCH A SAINTS GAME WITH A PRIEST

My tongue is still bleeding.

This is not to say that I am a person who uses expletives regularly in everyday life, but there are certain things about which I am ... ardent.

Among those would be the sports teams I support.

Understand that this was not a lifelong tendency for me. I have slowly grown to love sports. In the early days of my marriage I remember putting on short shorts, then negligees, and finally just rolling myself in bubble wrap to try to entice my husband away from a football game. But I ended up confusing the people who came to watch games with him and suffering from a plastic-induced rash.

In time I learned it was better to join than fight. So I'd find myself sitting for a few minutes in front of the Braves, maybe the Saints, or perhaps an LSU game, watching and nodding and smiling.

Time went on and little by little I began to notice things. What a well-turned double play looks like. Why fourth and inches can be pretty darn exciting to watch. Why any coach of an opposing team should be considered the anti-Christ.

The day the transformation was complete was the day I found myself at home screaming at the top of my lungs at a sight-impaired referee who made a ridiculous call against the Saints ... with my husband nowhere in sight.

But the good thing was it made me see how this attitude could be of benefit in other parts of my life. (Not the anti-Christ thing or the bubble wrap ... the watching the game thing...)

I realized that there were other things I had never been open to and that I might be missing something important.

If sports could have some useful purpose, such as the venting of anger and frustration in a method that didn't include road rage, semi-automatic weapons, or emails with emoticons, maybe there were other areas that had undiscovered benefits.

I went in search of other areas of life that I had not considered in the past.

I looked into hobbies. Like quilting. The thing I discovered about quilting was that it not only made use of things that other people found useless, but that it made me appreciate how joining different patterns together could make a beautiful picture. It was an incredible metaphor for the world – and just a little too deep. So I moved on.

I tried harmonica. My husband helped me in this hobby. Knowing my attention span or lack thereof, he bought a children's book for my harmonica lessons. Why do they think adults don't like cartoons, bright colors, and small words? Business books should be so delightful...

However, even a great book can't make a musician out of a person whose last musical masterpiece was *Twinkle Twinkle Little Star* on the recorder in junior high. I moved on yet again.

Okay, there were a few activities I still couldn't appreciate. Mime was one. I still want them to get stuck in that invisible box. NASCAR is one I'll have to work to understand. I heard that it's the nation's most-watched sport, but I still haven't figured out the fascination of left turn, left turn, left turn, cheer. I'll keep working on that one.

I guess that's the lesson here. I need to always remember that just because I don't get it, doesn't mean it's not there. So, I'll just enjoy saying a "Hail Mary" in penance after Saints games and wait to see when I feel it's safe to drive near a mime.

Now that's the definition of growth…

★★★★★★★★

> A I haven't trusted polls since I read that 62% of women had affairs during their lunch hour. I've never met a woman in my life who would give up lunch for sex.
>
> -Erma Bombeck

Chapter 74

LESSONS I STILL HAVEN'T LEARNED

Yes, it's already that time of the book.

Time for me to sit down and think about the many mistakes ... oops, I mean ... "learning opportunities" that I've encountered over the former pages.

These remind me that, whenever I start thinking I'm really smart and I know it all, it's time to think again...

- All the mistakes I've made have created the person I am today. And I like that person. So, I guess they weren't mistakes after all.

- If I keep introducing my husband as "my first husband," he'll never take me for granted.

- A person whose driving annoys me is probably driving the same way I do.

- Even on a bad day, I'm still quite useful at converting oxygen to carbon dioxide.

- Going to buy a "stud finder" at the hardware store is a disappointing experience.

- Curse words will not make unsaved documents reappear on my computer.

- Today my priority is sitting my bottom down and capturing thoughts on paper. The size of that bottom is a focus for another day.

- Life is too short to read bad books and too long to hold old grudges.

- Sometimes the greatest power is choosing not to use it.

- Some days I feel like I've really found myself. Other days I'm not even sure of my zip code.

- "We treat you like family" is not a good slogan for a restaurant. It would mean that they complain about how long it's been since you visited, notice that you've gained weight, and ask you to take out the garbage.

- Thinking that I know it all is the best evidence that I don't.

- Some days it's hard enough just to remember to close my mouth when looking up at the rain.

- If I say it in a book, I'm an author. If I say it in an article, I'm a journalist. If I say it in a sentence, I'm a teacher. If I don't say it and yet get the idea across, I'm a communicator.

- ✲ Some people call it "mowing the lawn." Others say "cutting the grass." I say it's a reason to buy a goat.
- ✲ For the sake of world peace and highway safety, we should all try to hide our smugness when we find ourselves at a red light next to the driver who zoomed past us earlier.
- ✲ If I accept that there is a name for my condition (ADHD, FMF, OCD), I seem more prone to use it as an excuse. I think I'll just stick with "crazy".
- ✲ When making a speech, it should be a law that no one can say the words, "And, in conclusion…" if they have more than three sentences left.
- ✲ If it's true that we all carry our own "weather", why do so many people insist on carrying tornadoes?

And finally, just like last year, I will forget every one of these lessons and have to learn them again.

When I saw a young college boy looking at me, I thought I was going to be like Mrs. Robinson in *The Graduate*. Instead, I was apparently more like Mrs. Kravitz in *Bewitched*.

Chapter 75

THE MORAL OF THESE STORIES

This is the point where I summarize this whole book into some very pithy bullet points.

I'm thinking.
Really, I am.
And I guess that's the point. There's no way to summarize life and explain it so that others don't have to stub their own toes. Even Aesop couldn't really help us, and he was a real writer.

The conclusion we can draw as we review the mishaps and haps in this book is this: Elastic is perfect.

- As a waistband, it loosens to allow us to focus on life's other priorities, but remembers its original size for whenever we decide to go back there.

- ✣ Like a rubber band, it can snap and remind us when we get too far off track.
- ✣ When used as a bungee cord, it can allow us to have our excitement, and then reel us back in.
- ✣ Like a mind, it stretches to encompass new information and pulls it all together so that it's always within reach.
- ✣ Like a heart, it can stretch to hold more love than we ever thought possible.
- ✣ And like friends, it ignores when we stretch it a little too far before we notice that we need to pay attention to it again.

And for that, we must thank Mr. Thomas Hancock and all of our elastic friends…

www.ingramcontent.com/pod-product-compliance
Lightning Source LLC
LaVergne TN
LVHW051547070426
835507LV00021B/2444